AF575146

CLASSIC MAGNOLIA ROCK

HISTORY OF ORIGINAL MISSISSIPPI ROCK AND ROLL 1953-1970

Frances,
I hope you enjoy this book as much as I enjoyed writting it

by

Johnny W. Sumrall, Jr.

Johnny W. Sumrall Jr.

AuthorHouse™
1663 Liberty Drive, Suite 200
Bloomington, IN 47403
www.authorhouse.com
Phone: 1-800-839-8640

First published by AuthorHouse 11/6/2008

ISBN: 978-1-4389-2960-6 (sc)

Library of Congress Control Number: 2008910156

Printed in the United States of America
Bloomington, Indiana

This book is printed on acid-free paper.

ACKNOWLEDGEMENTS

I would like to thank the following people for helping me with this book.

Robert (Bob) Thayer took pictures of many of the locations used by Bob McRee for recording studios. Some of these pictures are included in the book; others are being used to preserve the history of the period.

Sandy Ates made numerous trips to the radio station to make pictures of the guest artists so I could use them in this book.

Darden Wade gave me the opportunity to interview these artists on the radio and to play their music on air. This led to further research and the publication of this book.

Susan Sumrall, my wife, listened to many hours of records and interviews and helped edit this book. She encouraged me every step of the way.

The artists gave me their time to be interviewed and supplied pictures from their own collections for use in this book.

Bessie Cassedy Sumrall, my grandmother, whose 1938 painting of magnolias is used for the cover of the book.

INTRODUCTION

As I started writing this book, it brought back a lot of memories. I was only fourteen and everything was all right with the world. I lived in west Jackson at 200 Beach Street right off of West Capital Street in a two bedroom, one bathroom house with my younger brother, Tommy, and my parents John and Rheba Sumrall. Daddy worked and mom stayed home with us. My best friend in the neighborhood was Joe Traylor who lived down on Johnson Court. He introduced me to the first love of my life, Sherry Lea, one rainy summer day when I accompanied him over to her house. She called him that afternoon and told him she would like to go out with me. Later, I found out that he was dating her at the time.

I remember that Allen C. Thompson was Mayor and Hugh L. White was Governor; that segregation was in place; that the State of Mississippi was dry as far as liquor was concerned.

I remember going with my Dad over to Rankin County to buy liquor so my Grandmother Adams could make her famous Rum Cake for Christmas. We had to go down this gravel road almost to the Pearl River and drive up to this old shack. When we got to this shack a man would open the door and ask what we wanted and dad would tell him. He would bring it back in a brown paper bag and Dad would pay him.

I remember my Junior High School years at Hardy Junior High on Ellis Avenue; being on the track team and placing third in the state in the 220 and lettering. I also remember my best friends Armond Karow and Stephen Hood.

What I remember most from this time is discovering rock and roll music. It was the summer before I started senior high school. Up until this time there was only one high school in Jackson - Central High School. Two new schools were built - one in North Jackson (Murrah) and one in West Jackson (Provine). They were both college prep schools and Central was going to be a vocational school.

My Dad told me if I was going to start buying all this music that I needed to find some way to pay for it. He suggested a paper route. There were two papers in Jackson at the time *The Clarion-Ledger,* the morning paper, and *The Jackson Daily News,* the evening paper. I chose to deliver the evening paper. Soon, I started buying 45's, albums, and listening to the radio stations that played rock and roll. WJXN and WRBC were just a couple of stations that were playing the music.

Cliff Thomas and I were at Provine together and I found out the he was getting together with other musicians from Murrah and Central and playing at the VFW out at Hawkins Field and also at The Henry L. Graves American Legion Post at the edge of Hawkins Field on Bullard Hill Street. I started riding my bicycle to these places to hear them play because they were not very far from my house. I couldn't sing nor play an instrument but I was a good listener and loved to dance.

When I started to drive, I had to find another job to pay for gas, food, movies and dates. I started bagging groceries at Jitney Jungle on West Capital Street across from Poindexter Park. This is where I met the second love of my life, Henri Sue Dearing. My brother Tommy was also working there along with a guy named Bobby Tadlock. My brother Tommy started dating Bobby's sister Beverly. Since my brother did not have his driver license yet we had to double date if he wanted to go out. I don't remember how it happened but I started dating Henri Sue and we dated up until I was a senior in high school.

Now that I am through remembering for now, I will start this book by telling you it's all about the music. I lived this music growing up and I have gone back and interviewed the artists that I am writing about and this is their story through their eyes and their experience. I will try to give you some of my thoughts, as I deem appropriate as we start this journey together. Since a lot of this was going on at about the same time, the dates or order of importance will not be a factor in this book.

I hope you will have fond memories of the people and places discussed here.

–Johnny Sumrall

CONTENTS

THE RED TOPS

My earliest memories of The Red Tops were the stories my daddy told me when I was fourteen. He had a wholesale milk route in Vicksburg, Mississippi for Allen Dairy. He traveled to Vicksburg from Jackson; Mississippi on Highway 80, which back then, was a two-lane highway connecting the two cities.

The Red Tops were from Vicksburg and were well know in the area. One of the places where they performed on a regular basic was "Roger's Ark" in Bovina, Mississippi. This was one of my daddy's regular stops on the way to and from Vicksburg. "Roger's Ark" had one of the finest dance floors around. When The Red Tops played, they packed the house.

One of their most popular songs was a song written by a guy named Huddleston called "Swanee River Rock." They released a 45 record of the song. Had I known about it at the time, I feel certain that I would have bugged my daddy to get me a copy.

There was one other song for which they were famous - their version of "Danny Boy." Rufus McKay was the lead singer for The Red Tops. The other members of the band were: Willard Tyler, Joe Custard, Jimmy Bosely, Napoleon Flemming, Doc Raymond, Walter Osborne, Jesse Hayes, Lewis Spencer, Curtis Dunning, and Anderson Hardwick. The band was very unique in the fact they were playing rock and roll using saxophones, trumpets and trombones.

They also frequently played at Rosedale in the Mississippi Delta and at all of the state colleges. Some of the dances where they played were close to the state lines of other states that were not dry so that liquor would be readily available - all you had to do was go across and get your liquor and come back and party. Mississippi was dry at the time; this meant that liquor could not legally be sold or consumed in the State of Mississippi. If you wanted to drink you had to purchase your liquor from the bootlegger and disguise what you were drinking. The favorite form of disguise was bourbon and coke in a Dixie cup.

Although I never got to see them in person, my daddy said they were the best band around at the time. I did not hear "Swanee River Rock" until Tim Whitsett played it for me on a radio show I was doing about him. The Red Tops were a great influence on him in the type of music he performed.

I discovered later that Rufus McKay recorded two songs on a release for ACE records. When searching for old records in Johnny Vincent's warehouse I ran across a copy of it. The two songs were "Boll Weevil Junction" and "It's A Night For Love". I converted this into a CD and gave Rufus a copy when I saw him at a performance at Millsaps College in 2005 and he was thrilled. He did not have a copy of the record until that time.

Rufus left "The Red Tops" and joined "The Ink Spots." He sang with them for several years in Las Vegas. He is now retired and living in Vicksburg and occasionally performs with the Ben Shaw Band.

ANDY ANDERSON and THE ORIGINAL ROLLING STONES

"Andy Anderson and The Original Rolling Stones" started at Mississippi State College in Starkville, Mississippi (now Mississippi State University) in early 1953 because there wasn't any group on campus to play for student dances. The band consisted of Andy on guitar; Joe Tubb, lead guitar; William "Cuz" Covington on an old washtub bass; Roy Estes on piano; and Bobby Lyons was on drums. They practiced in their dormitory room until Joe Tubb, whose father was head of the Mississippi Department of Education, got a letter from Malcolm Grady, Head of Housing, saying they were having complaints from other students about the loud music. Dean Grady also mentioned complaints about having bird dogs in the room, but was more concerned about the music. Andy and Cuz were roommates and Joe liked hanging around with them so he moved in with them and slept on his mattress on the floor.

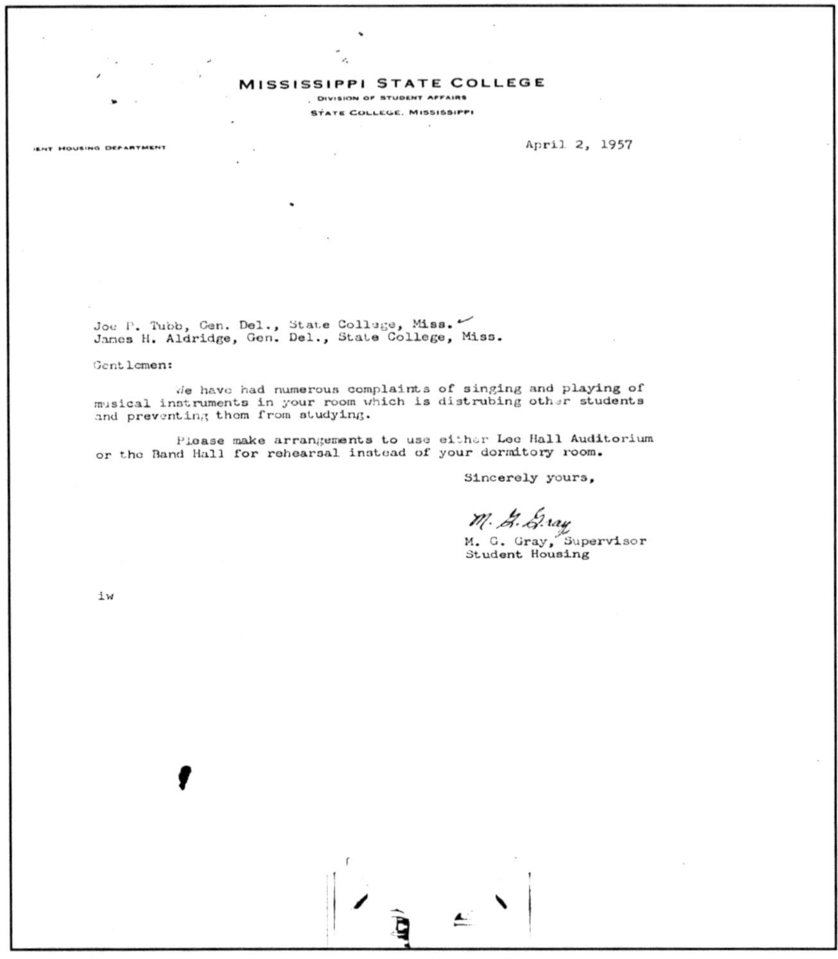

MISSISSIPPI STATE COLLEGE
DIVISION OF STUDENT AFFAIRS
STATE COLLEGE, MISSISSIPPI

ENT HOUSING DEPARTMENT

April 2, 1957

Joe P. Tubb, Gen. Del., State College, Miss.
James H. Aldridge, Gen. Del., State College, Miss.

Gentlemen:

We have had numerous complaints of singing and playing of musical instruments in your room which is distrubing other students and preventing them from studying.

Please make arrangements to use either Lee Hall Auditorium or the Band Hall for rehearsal instead of your dormitory room.

Sincerely yours,

M. G. Gray

M. G. Gray, Supervisor
Student Housing

iw

Letter from Student Housing to Joe Tubb regarding music practices in dorm room.

They decided on the name for their band one night after returning from "Crossroads," when Joe Tubb said they were just like the saying "a rolling stone gathers no moss." "Crossroads" was a frequent eating spot for them after a practice session. Thus they became "The Rolling Stones."

"The Rolling Stones" first paying performance was at The Southernaire Hotel in Columbus, MS at a dance for the students of Mississippi State College for Women. Then they began to play at Mississippi State and The University of Mississippi "Ole Miss" for proms and coming to Jackson, MS to play at The Legion Hut on Woodrow Wilson Drive.

About this same time Sun Studios in Memphis was getting started with such artists as Elvis Presley, Jerry Lee Lewis, Carl Perkins, and Johnny Cash. The band went to Memphis to try to get an audition and went into the studio. There they met Jack Clements and he invited them in and told them to bring in their instruments and set up and start playing. They started playing and noticed that they were being recorded. While they were playing, Jerry Lee Lewis came in and heard them and asked if he could play with them. Two weeks later Jerry came out with a song called "Down the Line" using some of chord changes the band was using when they played together.

The popularity of "The Stones" had grown and it had become too much for Andy and Cuz to try to manage. They entered into a contract with Jimmy Ammons of Delta Records and Mabel McQueen of Pine-Sol fame who managed the group for the biggest part of 1956.

'The Rolling Stones" parted company with Ammons and McQueen in order to go with a different agency who could get them more national exposure as their popularity continued to grow.

In 1957 the band entered the Mid-South Talent Contest in Memphis, TN and won. The prize was a recording contract with London Records thorough Murray-Nash and Associates. When they went to Bradley Studios in Nashville, TN to record their song called "Johnny Valentine" they were shocked to learn that they could not play on the record since they weren't members of the Musicians' Union. Andy could sing, but he couldn't play. The studio band was made up of Hank "Sugarfoot" Garland on lead guitar, Bobby Moore on bass and Buddy Holland on drums and the back-up singers were "The Jordanaires." The song "Johnny Valentine" was a spoof of a song by The Ames Brothers, "The Naughty Lady of Shady Lane".

"Johnny Valentine" became the first rock and roll record to be released worldwide. A slow song "I–I Love You" was getting as much airplay as "Johnny Valentine" and was the "B-side" of the record. The record was being heavily promoted in London, England and was getting a lot of airtime there. It was also very popular in Tokyo, Japan.

Later in 1958, the band came to Jackson, Mississippi and presented the Mayor of Jackson, Allen C. Thompson, with a copy of their record. They then had a parade down Capitol Street ending at Wright Music Company where they signed autographs. Later on that night they performed at The Rock House on North State Street.

Since the band members were not members of the Musicians' Union and couldn't play on their first record, they decided to cut their own record. Under the pretense of cutting a demo record rather than a record for release, they went into Bradley Studios in Memphis, TN and recorded "You Shake Me Up". Realizing that they did not have a flip side for the record, Joe and Andy went out to the car and in fifteen minutes came up with the song "The Way She Smiled". They originally wanted to do "Tough Tough Tough", but didn't want two fast songs on the same record. It so happened that "The Way She Smiled" had a female part to it and as luck would have it their manager had a girl under contract who happened to be at the studio at the same time and she sang the part. Apollo Records of New York released the record. It was instantly banned from the airways because of some of the suggestive language contained in the lyrics of "You Shake Me Up." But before it was banned it was picked as top pick of the week by Billboard and Cashbox.

Andy Anderson and The Rolling Stones

Left to Right: William "Cuz" Covington, Bobby Lyons, Joe Tubb, Andy Anderson

Left to Right: Allen C. Thompson, Mayor of Jackson, MS; William "Cuz" Covington, Andy Anderson, Bobby Lyons, Roy Estes, Joe Tubb (1958)

Andy and the other members of "The Rolling Stones" graduated from Mississippi State in 1957. Most of the band had earned degrees in Engineering and many had job offers in the business world. Bobby Lyons and Roy Estes both left the band for full-time jobs; Sammy Martina (piano) and Jimmy Whitehead (drums) replaced them after having served as subs for several years.

In December of 1959 at the height of "The Rolling Stones" popularity, Andy received a phone call from his dad telling it was time to come back and run the family plantation. Andy then returned to Clarksdale, Mississippi to run the family plantation. Howard "B.B." Boone took over the lead vocals for the band. "The Rolling Stones" continued to play, but lost some of its followings when Andy left.

Some of the things that happened to the band in their many travels follows, but in no certain order.

When they would play the Legion Hut on Woodrow Wilson in Jackson, Mississippi some future Mississippi rock and roll stars would come to hear them, namely Tim Whitsett and Cliff Thomas. There were others, but these are two that were remembered by the band as being present. If Andy Anderson or Joe Tubb dropped a guitar pick, these future stars would be scrambling to pick it up and keep it as a souvenir.

There is a story about a group of people that always traveled with the band no matter where they went. One of these people was Norman "Heavy" Quarles. He could always find the kitchen everywhere they went and usually took it over to make sure the band got fed. One time when they had an appearance at the Greenwood Country Club, a nice older lady showed Norman where the kitchen was. He saw that they were preparing finger sandwiches for the guests coming to the dance and decided that wasn't going to be enough to satisfy the appetites of the band. So he looked in the fridge and found some steaks and cooked them for the band. When it came time to leave, they were presented with a bill for the food. Somehow Norman stuck that nice old lady with the bill and the band didn't have to pay.

Another incident happened to them on the way back from a performance at the University of Alabama. It was late when they left Tuscaloosa and Jay Stricker was driving the car towing the rock and roll trailer. He was not in the band and had just come along for the ride. He started driving and got lost in a small town outside of Birmingham, Alabama and ended up on a dead end street and couldn't back the car up with the trailer behind it. So he decided to go to sleep and wait until the morning to wake up the band. The only bad part of it was that one of the band members had to be at work the next morning. When the band awoke the next morning they were upset they were still in Alabama. Needless to say, Jay didn't get to drive the car anymore.

After celebrating their win at the Mid-South Talent Contest in Memphis they were running late for a performance at The Annual Dairy Fair at Kosciusko, Mississippi. When they got to the high school, the person in charge directed them down to the football field where the performance was to be held. Andy was driving his 1953 Chevy station wagon pulling the rock and roll trailer and started doing figure eights in the middle of the football field for fun. During the middle of this little escapade, someone turned on the stadium lights and the stands were full of people. Needless to say, the band was more than a little embarrassed.

One time Joe Tubb and Jimmy Whitehead were at deer camp and were an hour-and-a-half late for a performance. Andy, like a real trooper was trying to play lead guitar, when finally Joe and Jimmy showed up. The band played an extra two hours to make up for the lateness of Joe and Jimmy.

They were always playing jokes on each other, and on the way to another performance Jimmy Whitehead had a cold and he asked the other band members if they had anything for a cold. One of the band members had some ex-lax and gave it to Jimmy telling him it was good for a cold, so he took two, which was a big mistake. He made many emergency trips to the bathroom during that performance!

And then there was Audrey Dale Petrie who bought an expensive saxophone so he could be on the stage with the band. He didn't know how to play a note, but he sure acted liked he could. "The Rolling Stones" had so many people traveling with them you thought it was full orchestra, when it was only five members in the band.

Another story revolves around "Bruno," a character the band created whom some of their fans will remember I'm sure. He had plastic buckteeth, a long black nylon wig with bangs, a crushed cowboy hat and a four foot stuffed snake. William "Cuz" Covington was the main one who wore this garb. Dressed as "Bruno," he would get the band to stop at a small town on the way to a performance and he would run down the main street terrorizing anyone and everyone he encountered. "Bruno" would run up to someone on the street acting crazy and punch the snake in his or her face. He was also known for going into restaurants with the garb on too. He wore it at many performances and on stage when the band appeared on "The Wink Martindale Show" in Memphis. There was a time that Martin Bittick wore it and ran down the streets of Clarksdale terrorizing three little boys and putting the fear of God in them. It is a wonder that nobody got arrested when they pulled this stunt.

Left to Right: William "Cuz" Covington as "Bruno", Bobby Lyons, Andy Anderson, Joe Tubb (Neshoba County Fair)

Andy Anderson

The first time "The Rolling Stones" played with Elvis Presley was in Walnut Grove, Mississippi at the Walnut Grove School. The drummer, Roy Aldridge, booked the concert for the band. While they were setting up at the school, a pink cadillac came driving up with a black bass tied on top, and out of the caddy stepped Elvis and Bill Black of "The Black Combo." This was right after Elvis had recorded his first record "Blue Moon of Kentucky" and before he became famous.

When the Rolling Stones would get an engagement they would tell all their friends. They would have as many as 20 or 25 people traveling with them to their performances. When they got there everyone would have to carry something in to keep from having to pay the cover charge. Someone would carry in an amp; three or four would carry in the banner that hung up behind the band. When it got time for the band to perform and it was only four people on the stage, the people putting on the performance wondered who the other 21 people were.

Andy had a 1956 Chevrolet that he had supped up with six carburetors. He tells the story about a time he, Cuz and Joe were headed for Greenwood and encountered some guys from Eupora who thought they had a hot car and wanted to race. They kept running up beside Andy and gunning their engine. Finally Andy let them pass him and he got right on their back bumper and pushed them until they were going in excess of a hundred miles a hour; then there was a puff of smoke from under the hood of the car from Eupora. Andy had made them blow their engine. Andy pulled around them and waved and proceeded on to Greenwood.

Andy was known to make wagers on his car, especially in some of the bars in the Columbus area. When the betting pot would get to several hundred dollars, Andy would drag race, win and take the pot.

Andy makes frequent trips to England where his music is still popular today. "The Rolling Stones" still play together along with some of the members of "The Dawn Breakers."

ANDY ANDERSON AND THE ROLLING STONES DISCOGRAPHY

Andy Anderson and The Rolling Stones
Murray Nash Assoc. BMI Felsted Records

Johnny Valentine (1958)
Andy Anderson (vocal), Hank "Sugarfoot" Garland (guitar), Bobby Moore (bass), Buddy Holland (drums) and The Jordanaires (back-up vocals).

I-I-Love You
Andy Anderson (Vocal), Hank "Sugarfoot"Garland (Guitar), Bobby Moore (Bass), Buddy Holland (drums) and The Jordanaires (back-up vocals).

Andy Anderson and The Rolling Stones
Buna Music Corp. BMI Apollo Records

You Shake Me Up (1958)
Andy Anderson (guitar and vocals), Joe Tubb (lead guitar), William "Cuz' Covington (bass), Roy Estes (piano) and Bobby Lyons (drums).

The Way She Smiled
Andy Anderson (guitar and vocals), Joe Tubb (lead guitar), William "Cuz' Covington (bass), Roy Estes (piano) and Bobby Lyons (drums).

TIM WHITSETT and THE IMPERIAL SHOW BAND

Left to Right: Tim Whitsett, Buzz Arledge, Hank Martin, Jimmy Hodo, Buddy Myers, Carson Whitsett. Bennett Jennings, seated.

TIM WHITSETT and THE IMPERIAL SHOW BAND

"The Red Tops," a musical group from Vicksburg, was the first real band that Tim Whitsett heard perform. They inspired him further into a music career that he was already committed to. It was before the release of the Red Tops first record "Swanee River Rock" that he heard them perform. He was in the eighth grade on an overnight Boy Scout trip to Vicksburg in April 1956 that he encountered the Red Tops. The Scout troop that Tim belonged to was camping at the Vicksburg Military Park. About midnight when the Scoutmaster had told them to get to sleep or face the firing squad, they got quiet. They heard the sounds that come out of the Mississippi night, the crickets and the screech owls, they became accustomed to the sounds and began to drift off to sleep.

Through the woods and up the hills they began to hear a strange sound. They asked each other what it was. So they crept out of the tent and worked their way through the woods to a hill overlooking Highway 80. There was a little dumpy club there called the Hill Top Club. The band that was playing inside was the Red Tops. They didn't sneak in because it was a black club and they were only kids and probably would not have been welcomed.

So they sat under the window and listened and stayed until the sun started coming up. They got back before the Scoutmaster woke up. After that night, Tim thought that's what I want to do and that is what he pursued.

By age of fourteen, Tim was forming his own band. He wanted to make records, but nobody had much use for someone so young with no experience. He looked up the address of Trumpet Records, which was a pretty big blues and country label in Jackson, Mississippi and went for a visit. It turned out to be a furniture store on Farish Street, a black area where the blues artists hung out. A lady named Lillian McMurray ran the company. Tim did not meet her at this time, but her husband advised him, in very strong words that were shocking to his young ears, never to get into the record business. Some of the artist that were on the Trumpet label were Sonny Boy Williamson and Elmore James.

In the late 1940's a new radio station came on the air, WJXN. Tim (about the age of 6 or 7) would pretend to be sick and stay home from school so he could tune in and listen to it. This was during the Korean War before Rock and Roll. On the station was a DJ called The Corn Poppin' Daddy. Tim was greatly influenced by this country music. It was around the age of 12 that Tim would listen to a black radio station WOKJ that featured Poppa Rock playing the current rhythm and blues. Poppa Rock would also rap the news and weather by hitting a pencil on the control panel while he read the news and weather.

Towards the end of 1958, Tim had already formed his first band, "The Deltaires" when he heard Andy Anderson and his group "The Rolling Stones" for the first time. Tim and the members of his band would go to every performance of The Rolling Stones when they came to Jackson. If Andy would drop his guitar pick, they would be scrambling to pick it up as a souvenir.

Tim still had a burning desire to make a record. In August 1960, Tim called The Singing River Recording Studio in Biloxi, MS and talked to "Prof" Carpenter. Marion "Prof" Carpenter was band director of Pascagoula High School and recorded for Decca Records as an instrumentalist. He told Tim that it would cost him twenty-five dollars an hour to have the master tape done. Tim had to figure out how to raise the money. About this time he saw an ad on the back of a comic book, "Earn money, sell Christmas cards". He went around to all of his neighbors pestering them to buy the cards from him. He finally earned enough money to pay for the recording session. Tim got all of his musicians together including Lane Cameron (Guitar),

Lee Graham (Bass), Jimmy Hodo (piano and sax) and Dulin Lancaster (Drums) and then talked Lane's mother into driving them to Biloxi to make the master tape of "Jive Harp" and "Pipe Dreams".

Singing River Studio was a primitive studio compared to today, but not necessarily primitive for the time. There were two one-track machines so that you recorded a track and over-dubbed it on the other machine. If you made a mistake anywhere you had to start all over again.

Tim brought the tape back to a local record producer, Johnny Angle, who listened to it and said he didn't think he would release it. This was a crushing blow to Tim so he decided that he was going to release it. He looked around and found that it was going to cost him about one hundred and twenty five dollars to press five hundred copies. Tim got the band a few jobs around town at local country clubs and high school dances. He was saving the money from the jobs and on his birthday, December 22nd, the band played for the dance that would give them enough money to have the records made. However, on his way home from the dance, he ran a stop sign and was stopped by the police. The ticket cost him thirty dollars and blew his budget. There were no more dances to play.

A friend of Tim's told him about a local jeweler, George Trebotitch, who was starting a record company. Tim played the tape for him and even though he didn't know a thing about music, George thought it was great and agreed to release it on the Trebco Label. Once it was released and began to get airplay around Jackson, Johnny Angle decided that it wasn't a bad record after all. Through his influence, the record was released to Imperial Records. This was quite an honor for Tim and the band; this was the same label that Fats Domino and Ricky Nelson were on.

After two members of Tim's original band went back to The Dawnbreakers Band, it became obvious that they would have to be replaced in order to release another record. At this time the band consisted of Murray Kellum on guitar and his brother Ronnie on bass, Carson Whitsett on piano, Jimmy Hodo on sax, and Dulin Lancaster on drums.

This was the first time that Tim's brother Carson appeared on a record with him. Carson played the piano on this record entitled "I Don't Care". Carson had been pestering Tim for a long time to play in the band; Tim had finally told him that if he could learn to play "The Flight of the

Bumblebee" without missing a note he could play in the band.

In the summer of 1961, the band returned to Biloxi's Singing River Studio to record their first record containing vocals. George Trebotitch traveled with them and was supposed to pay "Prof" Carpenter for the studio time – seventy-five dollars. George was one of those guys who was always "wheelin' and dealin'"; he just didn't pay cash for things if he could help it. He told "Prof" Carpenter that he would give him his watch instead of cash. Prof answered that he had a good watch and didn't need a second one. George listed all of the assets of the watch – it's brand new, it's Swiss, I'm a jeweler and it's my personal watch so you know it's the best. Finally Prof Carpenter said all right, I'll take the watch and walked out of the room. With that, George rolled up the sleeve on his other arm and took a watch off the replace the one he had just traded. It seems that George had a whole armful of watches!

The topside of this second record was "I Don't Care" which was Tim's first attempt at vocalizing. "Scalawag" the flip side was cut a month later in Jackson at Bob McRee's studio. Bob's studio was in a garage attached to his house on Ellis Ave. The echo chamber was a pit that he had dug to house his freezer. It was so dark that you had to have a flashlight with you when you climbed down into the echo chamber. The garage had split level doors. Through one door you got into the echo chamber and the other door led you to the control room. There were no lights in the control room so a flashlight was used to look at the meters and keep an eye on the recording levels. He had egg cartons on the walls to keep the sound in. Members of the band on this record were: Tim Whitsett, piano; Buddy Myers, drums; Murray Kellum, guitar; and Ronnie Kellum, bass. The record was released on the Trebco Label and became a number one hit in the Ft. Worth, Texas and Louisville, KY areas. It also charted in several other cities and was re-released by Atlas Records of New York. It was more popular than the first record that Tim had released.

It was also during this time that Tim began producing other artists' records. A group called "The Midnighters" who traveled with the Red Tops had caught Tim's attention. He located them in Vicksburg at a local grocery store and made a tape of them singing a-capella. He took this tape to George Trebotitch and convinced him to cut the record. They had to change the name of the group to "The Vels" because there was a group called The Midnighters already making records. Bob McRee's studio was used to record the group. One of the members of the group was afraid of the dark so they kept the flashlight on the whole time they were recording in the echo chamber. It was during this session in the summer of 1961 that "Please Be Mine" and "Mysterious Teenager" were recorded.

Tim wanted to get hired by Ace Records in Jackson and in February 1962 he placed a phone call. He knew that Frankie Ford had just left the Ace Label so he called Johnny Vincent's office at Ace and when the secretary asked who was calling, Tim responded "Frankie Ford". Johnny immediately came on the phone and said with an Italian accent, "Frankie baby, how are ya?" Tim said, no this is Tim Whitsett; your secretary must have made a mistake. Johnny said, "Aw, come on up, I have been wanting to talk to you anyway." Tim had written a song called "Olive learned to Pop-Eye" and told him about it. Tim played the tape that had been recorded in the living room of his family home. Johnny liked the tape and sent Tim and his band down to New Orleans to Cosimo's studio to cut the record with Tim's voice on it. However, when it was released, Scotty McKay was the vocalist with Tim's band. Tim's name was misspelled on the record, which only added insult to injury.

In September 1962, Tim decided that George Trebotitch was too much into his "wheelin' and dealin'" and parted company. Tim was ambitious and wanted to start his own recording label to complement his publishing company, Gulfway Publishing, and the Rim Label was born. During this time, everyone played on everyone else's record so it was whoever was available when it came time to record so the personnel varied. Tim ran the label on sort of a whim; he might decide he'd like to do a record like such and such and he called on whoever was around. He started using the organ because his lead guitar player went back to The Dawnbreakers Band. Tim had one of the first groups during this time to use an organ on records. He recorded most of the early Rim Record label recordings using Bob McRee's studio on Ellis Avenue.

The first Rim Record under Tim's own name was "All American Slob" which featured Tim singing. According to Tim it was really bad, but it was in the style of The Coasters or Huey "Piano" Smith.

Left to Right: Sitting Front Row: Tim Whitsett, Tommy Tate (on drum), Bill Dunlap
Standing: Bucky Barrett, Jimmy Hodo, Carson Whitsett, Eddie Jones (1967, Los Angeles, CA)

The flip side "Right Around the Corner" was in the Lee Dorsey style. The next record was an instrumental called "Mashville" recorded in January 1962. The flip side "Sweet Jelly" wasn't recorded until June 1962. They were both recorded in Bob McRee's second studio on Mill Street, which was right across from the train station in the back room of an old store. Tim and the band cut "Mashville" one night in January 1962 when it was about five degrees below zero – and the studio had no heat! The recording was very difficult that night. Tim played the organ because Carson was still in school and had to study. The flip side "Sweet Jelly" was recorded in June 1962 at Bob McRee's Ellis Avenue studio. The record was released in December 1962.

The next record has an interesting story behind it. There was a restaurant called Mack's Drive Inn on Mill Street, which was known as "Mack's by the Tracks" to Tim's fraternity brothers at Millsaps College. It really was built by the railroad tracks and was a real dive; the kitchen was in the middle dividing the white patrons' side from the colored patrons' side. This was during segregation and you could peer through the kitchen to see the folks on the other side. Tim's fraternity brothers would go down there late at night after a hard night of studying to eat and listen to the jukebox. To immortalize the place, Tim wrote an instrumental song about it "Mack's By The Tracks." The song was recorded at Bob McRee's studio in The Vincent Building in downtown Jackson. Lane Cameron stormed out after the session because no one told him his guitar playing was good.

During the time of Tim's first release on his own label, he was trying to get the local radio stations to play his records. One particular radio station, WOKJ, where Tim really wanted his records played, would not play them. Every time he took one of the records to them and played it for the program director, Jobie Martin, he was told that they liked it and would play it. Tim listened but never heard the songs. Finally, Tim asked Jobie why the records weren't being played. Jobie told Tim, "You have to be nice to me." Tim thought, I am nice; I'm polite and well mannered. Then a light bulb went on in Tim's head. This was the era of payola, but Tim didn't have the fifty or seventy-five dollars that the record promoters were going around the country paying the DJ's to play their records. Tim had an idea; he went across the river to Rankin County and bought a fifth of Ezra Brooks and took it to Jobie. It worked! His current record "Shine" became the opening number for just about every show and there were several dedications to Ezra Brooks. The flip side of "Shine" was "Mack's by the Tracks". It became a best seller in England and Belgium.

During the summer of 1963, Tim and some members of his band were on dates one night and decided to make a record on a whim. They went to Bob McRee's Ellis Avenue Studio and recorded "Little Liza Jane" using the girls as backup singers. Tim released the record as "Tim Whitsett and The Tootles".

Tim was always looking for new talent to record. During the MS State Fair in October 1962, Tim attended the show

"Harlem in Havana" and saw a great group performing on stage. Tim went backstage to talk to them only to find out that they were already under contract to another record company.

A little tap dancer in the show overheard him asking the group to sign a recording contract and said he would like to make a record. His name was Warren Cole, but his stage name was "Cozy Cole" and he was from St. Louis.

Tim said great because he wanted a rhythm and blues artist on his label. He signed him right there on the spot. To get him into the recording studio, Tim had to go down to the Royal American Show Train at the fairgrounds and pick him up. Tim took Cozy to Bob McRee's Mill Street studio to record the master tape. Tim put the record out; Cozy went off with the fair and Tim never saw him again. Tim had to change the name on the record label to Cozy Coleman, because there was another artist out using the Cozy Cole name, a drummer who had a big hit called "Topsy".

During the Summer of 1963, Tim convinced Johnny Vincent of Ace Records into letting him work for him as an un-paid employee cataloguing his records and listening to demo tapes that came in on various would-be

Left to Right: Buzz Arledge, Tim Whitsett, Bennett Jennings, Buddy Myers, Jimmy Hodo, Hank Martin, Carson Whitsett. (1965)

artists. Demo tapes from an artist in Mobile, AL came and Tim thought Johnny should sign the artist. Johnny said no that he had too many artists and didn't need anymore. Tim used Ace Records stationary to write the artist, Tiny Watkins, telling him that although Ace didn't have a place for him, there was a new record company in town, Rim Records, and they had heard the tape and wanted him to sign a recording contract with them. So Tim recorded Tiny Watkins and released two records, one being "Talk, Talk, Talk".

As previously mentioned, various musicians played on each other's records. Tim almost played on Murray Kellum's big hit record "Long Tall Texan", but as Tim put it, he had a "hot date" the weekend that Murray went to Memphis to the Pepper Studios to record it.

In 1967 Bob McRee, Cliff Thomas and Ed Thomas combined their talents and opened a recording studio in Clinton, MS called The Grits and Gravy Studio. It was here that Tim finally played on a hit record. They were doing the music track for a release called "Lovers Holiday" by Peggy Scott and Jo Jo Benson. Tim hit a wrong note on his trumpet right at the end of the track. He begged them to let him do it over, but they had several more tracks to cut that night. The song went on to become a national hit and won a Grammy – wrong note and all. The wrong note is still on the end of the song and Tim cringes every time he hears it.

In 1965 Tim and his band recorded a record called "Tia Maria" at Bob McRee's Nelson Street studio in Jackson, which was released on the major label Epic. Tim had four more releases after this one.

Tim continued on his musical career traveling around the United States with his Imperial Show Band. Toward the end of his playing career, he had a new lead singer, Tommy Tate, who was black. Tommy was with Tim's band from September 1966 until he and Tim went to Stax Records in 1970. They had been booked into a club at Lake Tahoe, Nevada and when the club manager realized they were a mixed group, there were grumbles. But the club let them play their two-week engagement. From Lake Tahoe, the band went to Las Vegas to play the Thunderbird Hotel. The Thunderbird let them play one show while they hurriedly looked for a replacement act without a black singer. The hotel paid them for the full engagement and the band went on to Hollywood where they did not experience any problems.

Tim worked at Stax Records as a music publisher where he listened to the demo records and tapes that came in. During this time, Frederick Knight kept sending demos and Tim kept returning them with his criticisms. Frederick finally got tired of this and made a tape singing in a high pitched voice and banging a piece of two-by-four on a stool as a sound effect. Tim liked it and Stax Records released it to become a national hit. It was titled "I've Been Lonely For So Long" and it became a million seller.

Tim later became president of East/Memphis Music Corp. In 1976 he resigned from East/Memphis when offered an opportunity to run Chrysalis Music's European division in London. After several years, Tim returned to the United States and founded Urgent! Records. The label's roster included Bobby Rush, The Dells, Luther Ingram, Tommy Tate and Jerry Butler. The label was later folded into the Malaco Music Group, with whom Whitsett became associated in 1998. In addition to his work with Malaco, Tim authored three music-publishing textbooks and a dictionary of music business terms, while actively maintaining his consulting services for music publishers and copyright investors.

As a publisher, Tim worked with song catalogues written by songwriters such as Otis Redding, David Bowie, Chuck

Berry, Isaac Hayes, Cole Porter, Irving Berlin, Rodgers and Hammerstein and many more songwriters.

Tim is back in Jackson producing and releasing records.

TIM WHITSETT DISCOGRAPHY

Tim Whitsett
Singing River Studio, Biloxi, Miss. 1960
Tim Whitsett (piano, trumpet, harmonica-1)
Jimmy Hodo (tenor sax, piano –1), Lane Cameron (guitar), Lee Graham (bass), Dulin Lancaster (drums).
IM 2990 *Pipedreams* Trebco 801, Imperial 5757
IM 2991 *Jiveharp –1*
(BB7.10.61)

Tim Whitsett
Singing River Studio, summer 1961
Tim Whitsett (vocals), Jimmy Hodo (tenor sax), Murray Kellum (guitar), Ronnie Kellum (bass), Dulin Lancaster (drums), Carson Whitsett (piano)
I Don't Care Trebco 703, Atlas 1253
(BB 27.1.62)

Tim Whitsett
Bob McRee's Studio, Jackson, MS, Oct (?) 1961
Tim Whitsett (piano), Buddy Myers (drums).
Scallywag Trebco 703, Atlas 1253
(BB 27.1.62)

Tim Whitsett
Bob McRee's Studio, Jackson, MS, 1962
Tim Whitsett (organ, vocals,-2, shouts), Jimmy Hodo (vocals,-1, tenor sax), Ed Clarke (vocals-1,bass), Lane Cameron (guitar), Carson Whitsett (piano), Dulin Lancaster(drums).
All American Slob -1 Rim 4102
Right Around The Corner –2

Tim Whitsett

Mill Street Studio, Jackson, MS

Tim Whitsett (organ, trumpet),Jimmy Hodo (tenor sax), Alton Lott(guitar), Wray Hixson(bass), Dulin Lancaster(drums).

9106 *Sweet Jelly* Rim 4105

Mashville Rim 4105

Scotty McKay with Tim Whitsett Band

Cosimo, New Orleans,La, May 1962

94-503 *Olive Learned to Popeye* Ace 652

504-504 Shame

Flip side: "Shame" session musicians from New Orleans

Tim Whitsett

Johnny Vincent Studio, Jackson, MS 1962

Tim Whitsett (harmonica), Carson Whitsett (organ), Lane Cameron (guitar), Lee Graham (bass), Dulin Lancaster (drums).

9853 *Macks By The Tracks* Rim 4107

The Vels with Tim Whitsett and The Imperials

McRee's Bomac Studio, Jackson, MS June, 1962

Mysterious Teenager Trebco 702

Please Be Mine

The Vels (vocals), Tim Whitsett (piano), Dulin Lancaster (drums), Murray Kellum (guitar), Ronnie Kellum (bass)

Tim Whitsett

McRee's Bomac Studio, Jackson, MS 1962

Tim Whitsett (piano,vocals,shouts), Carson Whitsett (organ), Jerry Puckett (guitar), Lee Graham (bass), Dulin Lancaster(drums).

9854 *Shine* Rim 4107

Tim Whitsett & The Tootles
McRee's Bomac Studio, Jackson, MS 1963
Tim Whitsett (piano, vocals), Helen Neyland, Catherine Hoffpauir (vocals), Jimmy Hodo (tenor sax), Carson Whitsett (piano), Jerry Puckett (guitar), Wray Hixson (bass), Dulin Lancaster (drums).
Little Liza Jane -1 Rim 4110
Lonely Clown-2

Tim Whitsett
Bob McRee's Studio, Jackson, MS 1963
Tim Whitsett (trumpet), Jimmy Hodo(tenor sax), Jay Stricker (tenor sax-1), Carson Whitsett (organ), Jerry Puckett (guitar), Ed Clarke (bass), Dulin Lancaster (drums).
879-879 *Monkey Man* –1 Ace 665
879-880 *Cotton Chopper*

Bubba Jordan with Tim Whitsett and The Imperials
Bomac Studio, Jackson, MS 1963
Guess Who
That's What I'll Do
released Oct 1963 on Buccaneer Records 501
Bubba Jordan (vocal), Carson Whitsett (organ-1, piano-2), Jerry Puckett (guitar), Wray Hixson (bass), Dulin Lancaster (drums), Buddy Myers (drums-2) Tim Whitsett (trumpet-2)

Tim Whitsett
Mississippi Artist Corp. Studio Jackson, MS 1964
Hank Martin (vocals), Tim Whitsett (trumpet, background vocals), Jimmy Hodo (tenor sax, background vocals), Carson Whitsett (piano), Fred Hawkins (guitar), Stuart Liles (bass), Dulin Lancaster (drums),
Randa Lowery
City Girl

Tim Whitsett

Bomac Studio, Jackson, MS 1964

Hank Martin (vocals), Tim Whitsett (percussion), Carson Whitsett (organ), Fred Hawkins (guitar), Guy Bowering (bass), Buddy Myers (drums), Jimmy Hodo (percussion).

I Would Cry Rim 4113

Peggy Paxton Hixson (vocals), Key Traylor (tenor sax), Tim Whitsett (organ), Alton Lott (guitar), Wray Hixson (bass), Dulin Lancaster (drums), The Del Sols (backing vocals).

Somebody Somewhere Rim 4113

Tim Whitsett and the Imperials Featuring The Turrible Bros.

(Tim Whitsett and Jimmy Hodo)

Mississippi Artists Studio, Jackson, MS 1965

Tim Whitsett (vocals), Jimmy Hodo(vocals), Carson Whitsett (piano, organ), Bennett Jennings (bass), Buddy Myers (drums).

Push Push Temporarie 000000

Don't Do It

The Imperial Showband

Mississippi Artists Studio, Jackson, MS 1965

Tim Whitsett (trumpet), Jimmy Hodo (tenor sax), Carson Whitsett (piano, organ), Fred Hawkins (guitar), Bennett Jennings (bass), Buddy Myers (drums, percussion), Jay Stricker (flute-1).

Tia Maria Epic 5-10005

Sad Wind –1

Tim Whitsett

Grits and Gravy Studio Clinton, MS 1966

Tim Whitsett (trumpet, flugehorn –1), Jimmy Hodo (tenor sax), Carson Whitsett (piano, organ), Ted White (guitar), Bennett Jennings (bass), Buddy Myers (drums), Tommy Tate(vocal-2).

Dees Village -1 Big Ten 1003

Stand By Me –2

Tim Whitsett and the Imperials Featuring Hank and Buzz
Mississippi Artists Corp. Studio, Jackson, MS. 1966
Hank Martin, Buzz Arledge(vocals), Tim Whitsett (piano), Carson Whitsett (organ), Fred Hawkins (guitar), Bennett Jennings (bass), Jimmy Hodo (glockenspiel, percussion), Buddy Myers, Dulin Lancaster (drums).
All I Need Rim 4114
Still A Lot Of Love Left

Tim Whitsett
Malaco Studio Jackson, MS 1969
Tommy Tate (vocals, drums), Tim Whitsett (tenor & alto recorders), Carson Whitsett (haprsicord, piano, organ), Bucky Barrett (guitar, bass).
Where Would I Go Musicor 1340
The Whole World Is The Same

RIM LABEL

4101 **O'Neal Hudson & His Sax Trio**
Blue Tango, September Song
4102 **Tim Whitsett**
All American Slob,
Right Around The Corner
4103 **Wendell Moore**
Send Me A Little Girl
Top Performance
4104 **Cozy Coleman**
Sad Joker, There'll Come a Time
4105 **Tim Whitsett**
Sweet Jelly
Mashville
4106 **Bubba Jordan**
Guess Who
4107 **Tim Whitsett**
Macks By The Tracks, Shine
4108 **Tiny Watkins**
Torturing Lover
All At Once
4109 **Joe Frank & Knights**
Palisades Park
4110 **Tim Whitsett**
Little Liza Jane, Lonely Clown
4111 Not Issued
4112 **Tiny Watkins**
Talk Talk Talk,
You Can't Take It With You
4113 **Tim Whitsett**
I Would Cry
Somebody Somewhere
4114 **Tim Whitsett**
All I Need
Still A Lot Of Love Left

CLIFF THOMAS

Cliff Thomas began playing with a lot of local bands in 1955, mainly because he had a guitar and amplifier. They played at the local VFW out at Hawkins Field in Jackson, MS, and The American Legion Hut on Woodrow Wilson also in Jackson and at various high schools in the area.

Cliff's brother Ed was going to Notre Dame and wrote their first song on his way home for a visit and called it "I'm On My Way Home". After they had worked on it some, they went to Memphis TN to the Sun Studios and did it for Sam Phillips. He liked it and decided to release it on the Phillips International Label. This label also had releases of Carl Perkins, Charlie Rich and various other artists. The flip side of "I'm On My Way Home" was "Treat Me Right".

Cliff went on to appear on Dick Clark's American Bandstand on the ABC network. Since there was not an ABC station in the Jackson, MS area, Cliff's parents had to make arrangements with South Central Bell, the telephone company, to hook up a television set in the basement of the telephone company to see their son on television.

It was also about this time that he got an invitation to appear on "The Alan Freed Show." Sam Phillips called him in December 1958 on a Friday and said he was to appear on the show the next day. Cliff caught a flight that night to Memphis and picked up Charlie Rich and went on to New York. When they got there they found out it was the next Saturday. They decided to rent a car and visit several record shops in the area and pantomime their songs and sign autographs. Charlie hadn't been out of Arkansas or Tennessee; Cliff had at least been to the Northeast once so he became the driver. So here you have a sixteen year old driving up through New England and surrounding areas to the various record shops. He finally appeared on the Alan Freed Show and preformed his latest hit record "Sorry I Lied". This record was climbing the charts; it featured a B3 organ on a record for the first time ever.

It was about this time that Jerry Lee Lewis married his thirteen-year-old cousin and shocked the world. As a result, all of Sun Records and Phillips International Records were pulled off of the charts.

Cliff did record one more record before he left the Philips label entitled "Tidewind." The flip side was "I'm The Only One". He did record one other record on The Ace Label. It was entitled "Shame" and it featured his brother Ed as a vocal back up. The label read "featuring Fats on the piano" in a reference to then popular artist Fats Domino, but it was really a studio musician named Allen Toussaint. The flip side of this record was "Do You No Wrong".

Cliff and Ed later began writing and producing records with another local songwriter, Bob McRee.

In 2007, Cliff released a CD, "Cliff Thomas" to celebrate his fifty years in the recording industry. Sadly for all of us, Cliff passed away in 2008.

CLIFF THOMAS DISCOGRAPHY

Cliff Thomas (Ed and Barbara)
Sun Studios, Memphis, TN 1957
Ed Thomas (Piano), Cliff Thomas (Guitar, Vocal), Ed and Barbara Thomas (background vocals).
I'm On My Way Home Phillips Label
Treat Me Right

Cliff Thomas (Ed and Barbara)
Sun Studios, Memphis, TN
Ed Thomas (Organ), Cliff Thomas (Guitar, Vocal), Ed and Barbara Thomas (background vocals).
Sorry I Lied Phillips Label
Leave It To Me

Cliff Thomas (Ed and Barbara)
Sun Studios, Memphis, TN
Ed Thomas (Organ, Piano), Cliff Thomas (Guitar,Vocal), Ed and Barbara (background vocals)
Tidewind Phillips Label
I'm The Only One

Cliff and Ed Thomas
Ace Recording Studio, New Orleans, LA
Ed Thomas (piano), Cliff Thomas (guitar and vocal), various studio musicians
Shame Ace Record Label
Do You No Wrong

Cliff Thomas Album (2007)
Festival Recording Studio, New Orleans, LA
Recorded live to mark the 50th anniversary of Cliff's recording debut at Sun Records, Memphis, TN, August 1957.
Cliff Thomas (keyboards), Mark Schloegel (guitar, vocals 12 & 17), Wayne Alley (drums), Jefferson Rodgers (bass), Myles Sharp (guitar, vocals 9), Rebecca Powers (vocals 3 & 15).

ANDY ANDERSON and THE DAWNBREAKERS

Things didn't work out with Andy running the family farm with his Dad, so he returned to Jackson, Mississippi and started a new band called "The Dawnbreakers." The members of the new band were: Buddy Myers on drums, Lane Cameron on guitar, Murray Kellum on bass and Charlie Stephenson on keyboards.

In late 1959 they had their first big hit on Century Limited Records entitled "Tough,Tough,Tough" backed with "Gimme Lock A Yo Hair". This created a snowball effect and led to four other hit records and a life on the road touring.

Andy Anderson and The Dawnbreakers

Andy Anderson in dark jacket; Lee Graham on left with back to camera; Lane Cameron on right. Laurel, MS.

The song "Tough, Tough, Tough" was an original song of "The Rolling Stones," but was never recorded by them, although they did play it at their many concerts.

There is a story that goes with the flip side of their record, that a drifter came through town with some new guitar licks, and approached Tim Whitsett and asked to play in Tim's band. Tim didn't have a place for him so he sent him to Andy. Andy used him on the flip side of their first hit record. This made Lane Cameron mad because he was the lead guitarist for the band.

The band toured for several years before Andy got the acting bug and went to Hollywood to try his luck. So the band quit playing and touring.

Here is a story that Andy likes to tell about "The Dawnbreakers" which involves Lane Cameron, Buddy Myers and Murray Kellum. It happens one cold winter night on a trip to a performance in Yazoo City, MS. Their regular trailer was in the shop having the wheel bearing replaced, so they had to rent a u-haul trailer with no top on it. For some unknown reason Murray Kellum had borrowed his dad's antique Ephiphone upright bass. As usual they were running late. Andy was driving his 1959 Pontiac Convertible up old Highway 51 North, which was a two-lane road and of course Andy was speeding. When members of the band began screaming that the bass had fallen out of the trailer, Andy thought they were kidding and thought they only wanted to stop and rest. Then he finally realized after much pleading that they were serious, he stopped, backed up the trailer and turned around. Sure enough there was the bass lying across the road on the centerline at a 45-degree angle. They jumped out of the car to get it, but there was a car coming and before they could get to it the car hit it and smashed it into a million pieces. The only thing left of it was the neck and the strings dangling from it. This old man got out of the car to see what he had hit and when he saw it he said “I done hit me a bull guitar”. Of course Murray was crying, trying to figure out how he was going to tell his dad about what happened. They did continue on to the Elks Lodge and play the performance. The band borrowed a bass for Murray and also took up a collection to help pay for the bass that was destroyed.

Andy and the band were on their way to Atlanta, Georgia traveling old Highway 80. They were traveling in two cars. Lane Cameron and Richard Thames were in Lane’s 58 Chevrolet convertible. Andy, Wray Hixson and Murray Kellum were in Andy’s ‘59 Pontiac Bonneville convertible pulling the rock and roll trailer. They were just outside of

Meridian, Mississippi, speeding as usual, doing about 80 or 85 with Lane in the lead. The road was elevated with steep inclines on both sides and it also was a two-lane road. They were headed for Tuscaloosa, AL when out of nowhere from a side road an old 1938 pick-up truck pulls out in front of Lane. He can't stop in time and all Andy sees is a cloud of dust and Lane's car going off the side of the road down into a bar pit. Lane hit the truck so hard that it was almost in a L-shape. The whole front of the truck was completely away from the firewall. An old man and a little boy get out of the truck unscratched. Andy and the rest of the band riding with him fear the worst. They all ran to the side of road and about the time they get there up comes Lane and Richard out of the bar pit. They were not hurt either. The only damage done to Lane's car was the front quarter panel. Andy asked the man if he had some insurance. He told Andy, "Yes sir, I got some burial insurance". Andy told him "good if you keep driving like that you'll probably need it." With the help of some people coming by they got the quarter panel pried away from the front tire and were able to drive the car to Birmingham, AL and leave it at a body shop for repair and picked it up on the way back from Atlanta.

In 1960 Ford Motor Company was furnishing the band with a station wagon and this story happened on a trip returning from playing at the University of Alabama. Lane Cameron was driving the station wagon and pulling the trailer. Andy was in the front passenger seat. Everybody was asleep except Lane who was driving, but he dozed off. There was a big noise as he drifted into the side of the 18-wheeler on a curve and this woke Andy up. The collision proceeded to eat up the whole left side of the station wagon before they finally got free of it. As Andy said that was the closest to death of all their experiences they had on the road; they could have met the 18-wheeler head on.

Another story that Andy tells is when they went to Baton Rouge for homecoming at LSU to play at a frat house on campus. When they got there to set up, the front yard of the house was being transformed into a pool. Sand bags were being placed around the front yard and surrounding sheets of plastic. They had built a bridge leading to a gazebo where the sweetheart of the Frat House could walk. The pool was to be 3 feet deep and they had a four-inch hose running up to the attic of the house connected to a flue to create a waterfall effect. Andy could see disaster written all over this. It was two hours into the performance that they started throwing everybody into the pool. The floor in the house had gotten so wet the band were getting shocked trying to play their instruments. Finally the band got some Coca-Cola cases to stand on so they could continue to play. When the frat boys threatened to throw the band into the pool, Andy told them they would stop playing and go home if they did; so they left them alone.

THE DAWNBREAKERS DISCOGRAPHY

Gimme Lock A Yo Hair (Anderson)
Century Ltd label 1960
Andy Anderson (vocals, guitar), Buddy Myers (drums), Lane Cameron (guitar), Murray Kellum (bass), Charlie Stephenson (piano).

Tough Tough Tough (Anderson)
Century Ltd label 1960
Andy Anderson (vocals, guitar), Buddy Myers (drums), Lane Cameron (guitar), Murray Kellum (bass), Charlie Stephenson (Piano).

Deep In The Heart Of Texas Rock
(Hershey-Swander)
Century Ltd label 1960
Andy Anderson (vocal, guitar), Buddy Myers (drums), Lane Cameron (guitar), Murray Kellum (bass), Charlie Stephenson (piano).

Chop Suey (Andy Anderson)
Century Ltd. Label 1959
Andy Anderson (guitar), Buddy Myers (drums), Lane Cameron (guitar), Murray Kellum (bass), Charlie Stephenson (piano).

BUDDY ROGERS

Buddy Rogers and I attended Provine High School, Jackson, Mississippi, graduating in the class of 1959. Buddy was a drummer in the high school marching band, but he also played in several local teenage bands in the area. I didn't know he could sing until I heard he was playing and singing at the Wagon Wheel, a club located in downtown Jackson. He was the first one in the group (Cliff Thomas, Tim Whitsett, Bubba Jordan and Murray Kellum) that I knew of that really sang soul music back then.

Cliff Thomas and Bob McRee recorded him on a song called "Waiting For The Sun To Go Down". On this particular record a saw and a piece of wood were used at the beginning of the record to represent the idea of someone working. This became the first use of a synthesizer on a record.

Buddy made another record also recorded in Bob McRee's Studio. This was an album of "Jimmy Reed's Greatest Hits" on a label that Johnny Vincent of Ace Records was using at the time. Buddy also recorded a 45 record for Bob McRee's Buccaneer record label. The first side was a Jimmy Reed re-make entitled "Tell Me You Love Me" the other side was a song written by Buddy entitled "Mad With You."

After talking with a fellow classmate of mine at Provine High School, Jimmy Jenkins, I found out that Buddy played with Jerry Lee Lewis at a concert in the old city auditorium in downtown Jackson, Mississippi back in the 1950's.

MARY ANN MOBLEY

Mary Ann Mobley (early 1980's)

I have known Mary Ann since before she became Miss Mississippi and then Miss America in 1959. She would come visit her aunt and uncle who lived next door to me at 200 Beach Street in West Jackson, Mississippi.

Sometimes when she would come over we would all load up and go to the movies.

When I interviewed her for this book she told me how she came to make a record with Jimmy Clanton of "Just A Dream" fame. Johnny Vincent called her not long after she had won the Miss America Pageant and wanted her to make a record with a nice young gentleman he had under contract. Johnny Vincent took her to the Cosimo Recording Studio in New Orleans where she met Jimmy Clanton and they recorded two songs for Ace Records - "Down The Aisle" and "No Longer Blue" which were released in 1961.

The songs were not that big of a hit. As Mary Ann laughingly said when I was interviewing her, she only knew of two sales - the one her mother bought and the one she bought. I told her I had a copy; so I guess that meant three sales.

She did tell me about making the movie with Elvis and what a perfect gentleman he was.

Mary Ann has had a successful career in TV and Film. She is married to Gary Collins and still spends a great deal of time in Mississippi.

MARY ANN MOBLEY DISCOGRAPHY

Jimmy Clanton and Mary Ann Mobley 1961
Cosimo Recording Studio, New Orleans, LA

Down The Aisle	Ace Records
No Longer Blue	

TOMMY TATE

It was a cold day in December of 1992 at radio station WZRX in Jackson, Mississippi that I first met Tommy Tate. I was doing my weekly radio show "Original Mississippi Rock and Roll" music. Tim Whitsett had played a song he had recorded by Tommy - a classic re-make of "Stand By Me." Cliff Thomas and Bob McRee also had talked about him and played several recordings that they did on him when they were on the show. I had contacted Wolf Stephenson at Malaco to track down Tommy to be on my show and now here he was.

Tommy was about eleven years when his music career started - playing the drums and singing. He was more interested in singing than playing the drums. It was at the Moonlight Inn in Pickens, Mississippi where he got his start. "Kid Butch" Rosby, a popular local bandleader of the time, was the first person to give him a chance.

Tommy actually started singing in church. Although he was a Methodist, his guardians were Baptists and he really liked the way the Baptists sang their hymns.

The singers that greatly influenced him were Ray Charles, Howling Wolf, Johnny Mathis and Nat King Cole.

Tommy first performance by himself was at Lanier High School, Jackson, in a talent show. He performed Richie Valen's song "Oh Donna" and won the contest.

He is the oldest of seven children and has a sister who sings along his mother in a gospel group locally in the Jackson, Mississippi area.

The first record he ever recorded was a song for Tim Whitsett. It was a B-side for a record that Tim and his Imperial Show Band recorded on the Big Ten Label. The A-side was "Dees Village" and Tommy's song was a re-make of a Ben E. King song "Stand By Me". This was recorded in 1966 at the Grits and Gravy Studio in Clinton, Mississippi and featured Carson Whitsett on the organ, Buckey Barrett on guitar and Bill Dunlap on drums.

This all happened while Tommy was lead singer with Tim Whitsett's Imperial Show Band. He traveled with the band all over the country and often encountered problems because of race and segregation. The band was a mixed group - it consisted of seven white boys and Tommy, a black lead singer. Performances were often cancelled when the makeup of the group became known; sometimes they were paid and sometimes not.

Another incident on this trip was the ticket that Carson Whitsett received. Carson's wife and new baby were traveling with the band to California for the next performance in his Studebaker Hawk. It was overloaded and had a muffler that was almost dragging the ground. Members of the band told him he needed to get that muffler fixed before he got a ticket. He said, "I'm going to wait until I get to California". As they traveled through Flagstaff, Arizona the State Police stopped him and gave him a ticket for the muffler.

The Imperial Show Band played locally at BJ's Lounge off Northside Drive in Jackson, Mississippi that was owned by recording artist B. J. Thomas. They also played at the Heidelberg Hotel in downtown Jackson after football games. This was where Tommy and Dorthy Moore would occasionally sing duets together and perform with the band. There was one song that the band would do called "Louie, Louie" that was so loud it would make the dance floor sway. The police would come in and make them stop playing because the dance floor was built over the parking garage and there was a structural problem.

One of the last records that Tommy did with the Imperial Show Band was a release on Verve Records. Since Verve Records already had a singer named Tommy Tate singing on their label, he had to change his name to Tommy Yates. The record was two songs written by the song writing team of Cliff Thomas, Ed Thomas and Bob McRee. One of the songs became a nice hit for Tommy entitled "If You're Looking For A Fool." Freddie Fender eventually recorded it on another label and it became a national hit. The other side of the record for Tommy was "Darling, Something's Gotta Give". This record was recorded at the Grits and Gravy Studio at Clinton, Mississippi.

There was one other record that was done about this same time by the songwriting team of Carson Whitsett and Tim Whitsett. It was released on the Musicor Record label. The songs were entitled "The Whole World Is The Same" and Where Did I Go?"

Tommy also recorded with an artist named Connie Davis from Gulfport, Mississippi. They used the name "Hank and Rover" and recorded on the Okeh label. The first song was written by Cliff and Ed Thomas entitled "A Lot To Be Done". The second song entitled "A Rock Down In My Shoe" was written by Cliff and Ed Thomas and Bob McRee.

Tommy went on to do many more recordings for Cliff Thomas, Ed Thomas and Bob McRee. He also became quite a good songwriter in his own right.

Tommy is still recording and enjoying the music industry.

Tommy Tate (left) and Johnny Sumrall with Tommy's album "*Tommy Tate*" (1987).
(Photo by Sandy Ates)

THE RED COUNTS

Martin Bittick, leader of "The Red Counts," got his start in music playing the piano in a band called "Jay Stricker and The Blue Jays" who started at Murrah High School in Jackson, Mississippi. They played at social teas and also played several times at the Governor's Mansion. Before he formed his own band, Martin played with The Rolling Stones when their regular piano player couldn't.

Martin traveled to Texas with The Rolling Stones to promote their first hit record "Johnny Valentine" where they were on the same television program with Brenda Lee, Fats Domino and Elvis Presley's Band who were still playing together although Elvis was away in the army.

A short time later, Martin formed his own band "The Red Counts" which consisted of Key Traylor on sax; Bubba Jordan performing vocals; Alton Lott on guitar; Ed Clark on bass and Richard Kersh Thames on drums. Later Alton Lott left the group and Cliff Thomas filled in until they found a permanent replacement. The replacement was Jerry Puckett. The group was playing at least two gigs a week and still going to high school. They were getting paid about twenty-five dollars a person for about four hours of playing time. This did not include the travel time.

They played as far away as Memphis, TN and Tuscaloosa, AL. The group also played in Bovina, MS at a place called Roger's Ark.

At the time there was only three white high schools in Jackson, MS; one county high school and several black high schools. Although they were from Murrah High School they did play at Central High School, Provine High School and Forest Hill High School on a regular basis. The counselors at the schools were involved in selecting the bands that played at the schools. The Red Counts had a very good reputation of not causing problems, and being non-drinkers. This helped them get a lot of the high school gigs. It also helped that the band's policy was that anyone that got caught drinking on the job would be fined $10.00, which was about half his pay. Martin Bittick the leader and manager of the band withheld $15.00 from each gig that he put into a savings account for emergency purposes.

At some point, Bubba Jordan left the group to do his own thing and he subsequently released two records. The band decided not to replace him because he didn't play an instrument - he was just a vocalist. And since he only sang ballads and slow tunes and everybody else could sing, they started letting Jerry Puckett sing the ballads and the slow tunes.

In an interview with Martin, he cited this incident as an example of the closeness within band. When they graduated from high school they all chose to go to Hinds Junior College in Raymond, MS. They were all majoring in music with the exception of one. It was the policy at the time that the entire class of freshman males got their heads shaved by the upperclassmen. A group of ten upperclassmen begin to chase Martin all over campus in an attempt to shave his head. They finally caught him, but he convinced them of the closeness of " The Red Counts" by telling them that there were ten of them, and they would track down all of the upperclassmen one by one and do more that shave their heads. He also related that they were still playing at the time and could I imagine seeing them up on the stage all with ball heads. Of course I could; it would have been a funny site. The ending of this story was they were the only freshman on campus with their heads not shaved.

Another incident happened to them on the way back from a gig on the Mississippi Gulf Coast. They were traveling north on Highway 49, late at night and pulling a U-Haul trailer covered with a tarp tied down with rope about the size of your finger. Martin saw flames and smoke coming from the trailer. Everyone was asleep except Martin and Key Traylor. Martin, who was driving, immediately yelled fire in the trailer and pulled off to the side of the road. He and Jerry Puckett started pulling the ropes loose trying to get to the fire to put it out. Richard Thames was not helping at all, he just kept yelling "save my drums, save my drums." He had saved up a lot of money and had a real nice set of drums, but of course they were in a fiberglass case and were in no danger of burning. Key Traylor grabbed his saxophone case out of the trailer, took it out, wet the reed and began playing "Harlem Nocturne" while Martin and Jerry were getting to the source of the fire. It was the blanket covering the speakers and amps. It seemed that someone had thrown a cigarette butt out the window and it had flown into a tiny hole not covered by the tarp and landed on the blanket and the wind had fanned the fire and caught the blanket on fire. It burned up the speakers and damaged the amps. Thanks to Martin's putting that $15.00 in a saving account after each gig, they were able to replace the speakers and amps for the gig planned for the next night.

After this incident, Martin and the band got together and had a custom trailer made. It was the first rock and roll trailer in the area. Andy Anderson and the Rollingstones had one, but it was not as fancy as this one. Soon all the bands in town had a trailer.

Martin left the group when he got married. The band kept on playing, but no one in the group took on the position of manager to replace Martin. It wasn't long before the band broke up and everyone went their separate ways.

RON FRAISER

In the early 1980's I was running radio channels one day, as I normally would do, and heard Ron Fraiser on the radio as a disc jockey. I got up enough nerve and called him and he agreed to be interviewed. I was delighted to tell him that I had a copy of one of his records. It was "Summer Skies" and "A Wish For Love" on the VIN Label. Ron wrote "Summer Skies" and Bubba Jordan wrote "A Wish For Love".

During the interview, Ron told about liking to write music. In the 1960's, Ron wrote some songs and sent a demo tape to a record company without copyrighting all of the music on the tape. It wasn't until several months later that he realized his mistake. He was riding the trolley in New Orleans when he heard his song "Hey Little Girl In A High School Sweater" being sung by Dee Clark. He called the record company and asked them about it; they said sorry there wasn't a copyright on the song so they changed a few words and released it. Ron said he learned a very expensive lesson from that experience.

Ron later recorded a 45-record for ACE records. It was a novelty song called "The Candidates Debate '76" which was a take-off on a presidential debate and used bits and pieces of other recordings popular at the time to simulate the debate. The other side of the record was a song written by Kay McNeely called "Lookin At The Sky."

RON FRAISER DISCOGRAPHY

Ron Fraiser
Vin Records 502
Summer Skies
A Wish For Love

Ron Fraiser
Ace Records 3017
The Candidates Debate 76
Lookin At The Sky

HARRY LEE (HUTCHINS)

I met Harry Lee one summer while I was still in high school when I got a job working for the City Of Jackson, Mississippi reconciling bank statements in the Accounting Department. As I reported to work that first day, there sat Harry Lee Hutchins - long blonde wavy hair sitting behind a desk working as an accountant. I learned that he was an accountant by day, a disc jockey for local radio station WJXN at night and also a singer and recording artist.

Harry Lee had two records out on the ACE Record label; both were recorded at the Singing River Studios on the Mississippi Gulf Coast. (The same studio that Tim Whitsett had used when he started recording.)

Harry's first record was a song written by his friend, Professor Marion Carpenter. It was originally titled "Linda, Linda" but the name was changed to "Lynda, Lynda" to honor Lynda Lee Meade, Miss Mississippi who had just won Miss America in 1960.

Marion Carpenter also wrote the other 45's Harry Lee recorded. They were entitled "Looking, Seeking, Searching" and "Are You Real." Professor Carpenter was the owner of Singing River Studios and had at one time worked for DECCA Records.

Harry also teamed up with Alton Lott and recorded two songs written by him. Alton played on Harry's final record on the Vin Label entitled "You Don't Know" and "Every Time I See You. The Vin Label was a label that Johnny Vincent used from time to time in addition to his Ace label. He also recorded two more songs on the Vin Label one written by Marion Carpenter entitled "Undertow" and one he wrote called "Hair Of Gold". This was released in May of 1959 before the two previous songs on the Vin Label, which were released in July of 1959.

I ran into Alton and asked him what ever happened to Harry Lee and he was like everybody else that I have asked - nobody seems to know.

AL WARD

Al Ward started in the music business at age twelve in a small town in North Carolina. His brother Frank played the guitar in a band that played for a local square dance on Saturday nights. One Saturday night Frank let Al sing the only song he knew, "Home;" he was so good that he sang it every Saturday night.

When Al was fourteen they moved to Concord, North Carolina a few miles from where he previously lived. There he started singing with "The Jack Ely Band", and again it was Frank who got him started by convincing Jack that Al could sing the Bing Crosby arrangement of "It's Been a Long, Long Time". Jack Ely had his own radio show in Concord and Al became a regular on the show. The saxophone player in Jack's band was Bob Simpson, who was an executive for Cannon Mills, and he got Al hooked up with "The Billy Canuff Band" who played mostly in New York.

While Al was in New York he hung out at a drug store on Broadway where a lot of the young artists would meet. There he met Bobby Darin, who had just recorded his big hit "Splish Splash", based on an idea given to him by his mother-in-law, Sandra Dee's mom. He told Al it was the wildest thing he had ever recorded.

Al later joined the Air Force and stayed in for many years. When he got out of the Air Force, he went to the Mississippi Gulf Coast on a fishing trip. One day while he was there, it was too rainy to go fishing and he was watching Mobile, Alabama's channel 3 on TV. There he saw a show called "The Toast of the Coast" hosted by Ross Smitherland. Ross was telling everyone watching that he really needed some talent on his show and they could call a certain number to arrange for an audition. So Al called and went for an audition and got on the show. He decided to stay on the Coast.

Al began to perform at the Azalea Grill in Mobile, AL around 1956. He worked with a group called the "Novel Aires" for a time, then moved to Pensacola, Fl and sang at a club called the "Skylark".

He returned to Mobile and started working at a restaurant called "Martine's" and would sing two or three songs every hour. Al thought that he wasn't earning his paycheck and should be doing more, so he approached the owner, Nick Galva, with the idea that he should meet the guests at the door and help them get seated and ask them what songs they would like to hear. As in any business, especially the music business, there were always people who told you what they were going to do for you, but it never materialized. One night a man approached Al and told him all these things that he was going to do for him and gave him his business card and told Al to call him. Al proceeded to tell Nick about it and showed him the card. Nick told Al that Dumas Milner was the largest automobile dealer in Mississippi and was a man of his word and that Al should call him. Al did and Mr. Milner sent airplane tickets for a flight on Southern Airways to Jackson, MS where he arranged an audition with people from New York's Mercury Records. Al came into the room and had to sing without accompaniment. He then was asked to leave the room while they discussed it. When he came back into the room, Dumas Milner offered him a contract, with all expenses paid, and he could keep half of what he made. Al signed the contract. Dumas Milner had just bought radio station WJQS in Jackson, Mississippi and wanted to use Al's talent. The new station manager was Lou Halbrenner, from North Carolina. He and Al hit it off; especially since both of them were from North Carolina. Lou asked him what his job was and Al told him that he was a singer who also played the guitar. Lou then developed a program around Al and called him the "Young Mister X" and teamed him up with Skeet McWilliams on guitar and Wally Albeit on piano.

After a few months Dumas Milner sent Al to New York to study voice with Fred Steele, who was a voice coach for Steve Lawrence and Eydie Gorme. With Fred leaning back in his chair with his pipe in his mouth, Al started the audition. Al thought that he was making a good impression until he quit singing and Fred said that he had enough talent to work with and that Al needed more vocal training; but he would work with Al three times a week for forty-five minutes if Al could keep up; if not he would drop him down to twice a week. Mr. Milner was anxious to get Al on the road and encouraged him to keep up which he did. Soon Al began to sing with "The Jimmy Palmer Band" that was appearing at the Roseland Ball Room in New York.

It was while he was in New York that Al made his first and only recording. It was on the "Big B" label, a subsidiary of Mercury Records. Al was twenty-seven years old at the time. His friend Lou Halbrenner was his personal manager and brought him a song by a friend of his from New Orleans, LA. The song was entitled "Tell Her Mister Moon" which became the "A" side of the record; the "B" side of the record was "For You My Lover". During this time the music was recorded first and the singer came back and sang the vocal. The record went on to sell over two thousand copies which was quite an accomplishment in the late 1950's and the trade magazines gave both sides of the record the highest rating in years. The "B"side "For You My Lover" won the Italian Music Award. Al began a DJ tour of the U.S. promoting the record.

Louise Yeager a public relations person who had an office in the King Edward Hotel in Jackson, Mississippi, knew the wife of Jim Hobbs, the producer of "The Lawrence Welk Show", and sent her a copy of the record. Jim Hobbs liked it and got Al on the show within two weeks time - it usually took months to get on. Al was on a DJ tour in Ft. Worth, Texas when he was notified he was going to be on "The Lawrence Welk Show". Mr. Welk made the comment to Al that he "talked like a Rebel but sang like a Yankee."

After the DJ tour, Al returned to Jackson, MS where he has taught guitar and voice for many years.

GLENN SUTTON

Glenn came to Mississippi from Hodge, Louisiana, where he was born in 1937, and started working in the Jackson area as an insurance salesman. This is where he met Bob McRee and most importantly Murray Kellum. Glenn was a guitar player and a songwriter. He began playing in Murray's band and Glenn went to Memphis with Murray when he recorded his big hit "Long Tall Texan". Since Murray didn't have a song to put on the B-side, Glenn recorded one of his entitled "I Gotta Leave This Town". The record was released in 1963. It stayed eleven weeks on Billboards Record Charts. It started at number 62. The highest it got was number 51.

Glenn later teamed up with Bob McRee and wrote a song entitled "Ring On Your Finger" which he recorded for ACE records. The B-side of that record was also another song written by Bob and Glenn entitled "Don't Have You". It wasn't long after that, Glenn left for Nashville to seek his fame and fortune. There he found an audience for his song writing talents and became a very successful country songwriter. He had a long association with Billy Sherrill that led to many hit tunes over the decades. Glenn was married to Lynn Anderson, the country music singer, and produced her big hit "I Never Promised You

A Rose Garden". The marriage ended in divorce. The rest is history.

Royce Glenn Sutton was elected to The Songwriters Hall of Fame in Nashville in 1999. Glenn passed away April 17, 2007.

JAY STRICKER and LANE DINKINS

The following two people, although not recording artists in their own right, did appear on several records.

Jay Stricker got his start through his daddy's influence. His daddy took him to New Orleans on the weekend at an early age to hear the great musicians play their clarinets and saxophones. This influenced Jay to take up the clarinet very early. He formed his first band while in the seventh grade. Jay's first band was called "Jay Stricker and The Blue Jays." His grandmother would get the band engagements at the Governor's Mansion for social teas. Some members of his early band were Martin Bittick and Key Traylor.

Later on when he got his driver's license, Jay bought a 1948 Pontiac convertible and put a sign on the doors saying, "Jay Stricker and His Orchestra - For bookings call this number." He drove all over town and didn't get a single call.

Jay told me of playing one time in Yazoo City at a club that had two gas pumps out front. The band members felt they needed a bodyguard at this establishment; so they recruited Hugh Shearer also known to many as "Baby

Huey" who was an outstanding football player at Central High School in Jackson. Jay promised him ten dollars to sit on the stage while they performed. Although nothing happened that night, they felt comfortable having him there. Jay says he never paid him the ten dollars and every time Jay sees Hugh he reminds him of the amount still owed to him.

After high school, Jay enlisted in the Marines and after his tour of duty returned to Jackson. Bob McRee wanted him to become a studio musician in his recording studio. Jay started playing at the Grits and Gravy Studio in Clinton, Mississippi where Bob had gone in business with Cliff and Ed Thomas. This was where Jay played flute for the first time on a record. It was entitled "Hideway" by The Tams.

As Jay put it during the interview, this was the dark ages and they recorded the music track and the singer or singers would come in and record the voice track. They would start recording the music track and if someone would hit a wrong note they would have to start over. He remembered one such time it took them 17 hours to record one music track and the poor guy playing the trumpet's lips became very swollen.

Jay went on to play frequently as a fill-in for local bands and traveled some with Andy Anderson and The Dawnbreakers.

In the late 1950's-early 1960's, the only bands playing locally were "Tim Whitsett and The Imperial Show Band" and "Andy Anderson and The Dawnbreakers." It was during this time that Lane Dinkins joined Bobby Bennett's band, "The Esquires" while going to Murrah High School in Jackson, Mississippi. "The Esquires" began playing dances after high school football games; soon they were playing college dances all over the South. "The Esquires" first record release was in 1961. The A-side was "Smoke Rings" and the flip side was "Licorice Stick."

"The Esquires" almost became famous when Bobby Bennett wrote a song called "Smoking Is Bad For You." It came out at the same time the Surgeon General issued his report about smoking being bad. Someone from CBS heard the record and the network sent a crew from New Orleans to video tape the band lip-syncing the song so it could be aired on the Mike Wallace Morning News program on CBS. The band was also scheduled to appear on the cover of Life Magazine. Just when they were ready to go out and buy a whole stack of the magazine, they found a musical group from England called "The Beatles" had bumped them from the cover.

Lane played for several years as a drummer for various groups around town, but now is retired from playing.

ALTON LOTT

I was introduced to rock and roll music on a summer evening in 1956. I was riding my bike in the neighborhood when I heard a guitar being played at Diane Bunyard's house. Later, I learned that it was Alton Lott who was playing. Diane and Alton were dating at the time even though she went to Jackson's Central High School and Alton went to Forest Hill High School. Alton graduated from high school in 1958.

Alton's whole family was musical so it was only natural that he became a musician and a singer. His cousin, Jimmy, moved in with Alton's family after being discharged from the Navy and Alton and Jimmy began performing at dances, on televised telethons, radio shows and in clubs.

"Alton and Jimmy" as they were called began writing songs together. After auditioning for Johnny Vincent's Ace Record Company in Jackson, MS, they cut two songs entitled "Looking For Someone" and "Got It Made In The Shade" in 1958 at the Cosimo Recording Studio in New Orleans, LA. Huey "Piano" Smith, who had a big hit with "Rockin' Pneumonia and Boogie Woogie Flu" on Ace, played piano on this session.

Jimmy was recalled back into the Navy so Alton began touring with several other artists and was a studio musician for many years. He played live performances with Andy Anderson, Murray Kellum, Buddy Rogers, and B.B. Boone and also played on Murray Kellum's record "Brand New Baby."

Alton also wrote and played on two songs that were released by Harry Lee on VIN records entitled "You Don't Know" and "Every Time I See You."

Later Alton joined "Faux Pas" band and spent 14 years touring the U. S. playing all the major cities.

He is now retired and living in Kansas City, MO. He occasionally returns to Jackson, MS to play with the original Rolling Stone Band when they get together.

JOHNNY VINCENT

Johnny Vincent Imbragulio was born in Hattiesburg, Mississippi. He moved to Jackson, Mississippi in the late 1940's where he opened a record shop and started the Champion Records label in the early 1950's. Johnny worked with Specialty Records for a while before he left and formed his own label, Ace Records, in 1955.

Johnny originally planned to name his recording label "Capital" but there was a company using the name "Capitol." Due to the fear of being sued by the larger company because the names sounded so much alike, Johnny had to choose another name for his company. He went to the drugstore to think and saw a display of combs bearing the brand name ACE and decided that would be a perfect name. It was short, memorable, and more importantly, at the first of the alphabet so he would get paid first by record stores where he had his records on consignment.

Johnny's first big record on Ace was the song "Don't You Just Know It" by Huey "Piano" Smith. The song was very popular in the New Orleans area. A radio DJ in New Orleans knew that the American Broadcasting Company (ABC) was just starting in the record industry and he called ABC to recommend the song to them. ABC called Johnny and requested that he come to New York to discuss putting the record out on their label. Johnny refused their offer of a fifty thousand dollar ($50,000) advance and refused to do business with them. This greatly irritated ABC who said they would make certain that the song would never be played on "Dick Clark's American Bandstand."

On his trip home from New York, Johnny went to Philadelphia, PA to see Dick Clark. Due to the dozens of record label representatives present, Johnny had to wait his turn. When he got in to see Dick Clark, he told him what had happened in New York and how he was just a small record label in Mississippi trying to make a living. Dick Clark was quick to tell Johnny that he worked for the television station in Philadelphia and not ABC and they could not tell him what he would or would not do. Dick Clark called in his producer and said this is the record that they would play and not any other releases of the song. After that, anything on Ace Records that Johnny sent to Dick Clark got played on "American Bandstand." This exposure helped Ace Records have many million-selling records.

Some of the national hits recorded during the late 1950's included Huey "Piano" Smith's "Rockin' Pneumonia and Boogie Woogie Flu;" Jimmy Clanton's "Just A Dream" and Frankie Ford's "Sea Cruise" among others.

In 1960, Johnny decided that he should record Mary Ann Mobley and Jimmy Clanton doing a sweetheart record. Mary Ann was Miss America and Jimmy was one of the new teenage heartthrobs so Johnny thought they would make the perfect "couple." Johnny contacted Mary Ann and she agreed to sing the duets with Jimmy. The two songs were "Down the Aisle" and "No Longer Blue."

At this same time, Jimmy was named to be the lead in the movie "Teenage Millionaire" and the female lead role was offered to Mary Ann. Johnny said that Mary Ann turned down the part because she wasn't offered enough money.

Johnny Vincent recorded quite a few local Jackson artists including Harry Lee, Ron Fraiser, Mary Ann Mobley, Cliff Thomas, Buddy Rogers and Rufus McKay lead singer of The Red Tops.

Johnny was also a great influence on Tim Whitsett getting him starting in the recording business.

In 1962, Johnny Vincent closed down the label due to the difficulties of distribution for a small independent label. He reactivated the label in 1971 to produce some new music and reissue some of the treasures from the label's storehouse and to lease the masters to other labels.

I remember meeting Johnny through my friend Darden Wade when I was doing my radio show at WZRX in Jackson in the late 1980's. I found out that Johnny had two warehouses of records and I asked him if I could go through those warehouses looking for records for my collection. He agreed and for several Saturdays my youngest son Adam, my friend Bill and I went through these warehouses looking for old records. I found many records to add to my collection and will forever be grateful to Johnny Vincent for his willingness to share with me.

Johnny Vincent Imbragulio passed away in February 2000.

BOB McREE'S RECORDING STUDIOS

The first known recording studio in Mississippi was Professor Carpenter's Singing River Recording Studio on the Mississippi Gulf Coast in the early fifties.

Bob McRee started his first studio in Jackson in the late fifties while still in school at Provine High School. The studio was on Ellis Avenue, just off of West Capital Street. He started it with a 4-track recorder in the family garage with egg cartons nailed to the walls for soundproofing. A hole dug in the floor where a freezer once stood served as an echo chamber. As noted, Bob didn't have any fancy equipment, but he did have a good ear for sound. One of the first recordings he made was of a group called "The Vels" that Tim Whitsett brought to him. They were a group that opened for "The Red Tops" out of Vicksburg, Mississippi. To get the sound that they wanted, the lead singer for "The Vels," who was afraid of the dark, was given a flashlight while recording from the echo chamber.

Bob later opened an additional recording studio on Mill Street in Jackson, Mississippi. It was located in a building with a storefront facing the train station in downtown Jackson. He used the back room for the recording studio. If a train was passing by, they would have to stop recording until it left. He also continued to use the Ellis Avenue Studio, which he had named the Bomac Studio.

Tim Whitsett tells a story about the night he and Jimmy Hodo were out on a date with their favorite girls at the time whom they wanted to impress. So they decided to cut a record. They went to Bob's house on Ellis Avenue and recorded "Little Liza Jane" with the girls singing back-up vocals.

Bob was constantly moving his recording studio and in the early 1960's he opened one on O'Farrell Street in West Jackson. This is where Dorothy Moore started recording for him. It seems that Cliff Thomas would pick her up from high school and bring her to the studio to record. It was also at this time that Cliff and his brother Ed starting writing songs with Bob. They would find local artists to sing their songs; record them; and then lease the recorded songs to various labels thorough out the United States. One such record was a release by Dorothy Moore and a group of girls from Jackson State. The group was called "Dorothy and The Hesitations." Both sides of the 45 record were written by Ed Thomas. The songs "Trying To Work A Plan" and Don't Set Me Up (For The Kill)" were leased to Jamie Records.

Prior to this, Bob had a few releases on his own Buccaneer label. One was by local artist Buddy Rogers. The songs were "Tell Me You Love Me" and "Mad About You". Another local artist that Bob recorded was Bubba Jordan. He recorded "Guess Who" and "That's What I'll Do". Bob then recorded a group out of New Orleans called "Bob Runnel's Faux Pas III." They recorded two of Ed Thomas's songs "Where's Willie Walker" and "For My Baby".

For a short time Bob had a recording studio in the Vincent Building in downtown Jackson. This was the home of Ace Records at the time.

He then teamed up with Cliff and Ed Thomas and purchased an old movie theater in Clinton, Mississippi and started "The Grits and Gravy Studio." Out of this studio came many successful records. One that won them a Grammy in the rhythm and blues category "Lover's Holiday" was sung by Peggy Scott and Jo Jo Benson. Another popular song done by this duo was "Pickin' Wild Mountain Berries". As the story goes, Tim Whitsett played the trumpet on "Lover's Holiday" and hit a wrong note at the very end and they wouldn't redo the music track to correct his wrong note. So every time he hears that song he cringes at the sound of the wrong note at the end.

Another song that was recorded at the "The Grits and Gravy Studio" was sung by Tommy Tate "If You're Looking For A Fool." It was written by Bob, Cliff and Ed and leased to Verve Records. Another artist, Freddy Fender, eventually recorded this song which went on to be a big hit nationwide. The band backing up Tommy on this record was "The Imperial Show Band," Tim Whitsett's band.

BOB McREE, CLIFF THOMAS and ED THOMAS SONG WRITERS and RECORD PRODUCERS

Cliff Thomas graduated from Provine High School in Jackson, MS in 1959 and left to attend Georgia Tech in Atlanta, Georgia. He was active in the music business while in college, playing in bands in the Atlanta area. He also signed a record and management contract with "The Atlanta Tams," a local group. While in Atlanta, Cliff became associated with Bill Lowery who was managing the 123 Label for Capitol Records. Upon graduation from Georgia Tech, Cliff sold the contract he had on "The Atlanta Tams" to Bill Lowery and returned to Jackson.

Once back in Jackson he joined the family business, Norman Shirt Manufacturing. He joined with Bob McRee and his brother Ed to start Grits and Gravy recording studio in Clinton, MS. They received a little help from Huey Meux, a record producer from New Orleans known as the "Crazy Cajun." They bought the old Hill Top Movie Theater close to Mississippi College, a private Christian school. Cliff, Ed and Bob started writing songs together. They used Bob's talent to record the songs and they made a great team.

Their first big record was a duet by Peggy Scott and Jo Jo Benson. Huey Meux discovered Peggy and Jo Jo and brought them in to record. Tim Whitsett played trumpet on this record and hit a wrong note at the very end of the music track and begged them to do it over. They were cutting a bunch of tracks that night and told him no one would notice that wrong note. Back then they cut the music tracks first and then they brought the vocal singers in next to sing. The first big record was "Lover's Holiday" and was released on the SS International label a division of Shelby Singleton Productions.

While Peggy and Jo Jo were in town, Cliff, Ed and Bob decided to come up with another song for them to sing. Bob came up with an idea the next morning while sitting at the breakfast table with his parents. They had run out of jelly for their toast and his father asked him to reach up above the refrigerator and get a jar of strawberry jelly. This made Bob come up with the song title "Pickin' Wild Mountain Berries." When he got to the recording studio that morning he told Ed and Cliff about the song title. They proceeded to write the song to fit the title. It also became a big hit for them.

Bob was still using his 8-track recorder to record. In order to have an echo chamber he had to send the sound outside through an air duct and back into the building to record it. Birds were bad about getting into the air duct and on several occasions he had to send someone outside to chase the birds out of the air duct.

Another group that they recorded was "The Sugar Blues" from Duck Hill, MS. Duck Hill is a small town in north Mississippi and when The Sugar Blues would perform they would close down the whole town to hear them. Ed Thomas wrote two songs for them "Look What We Have Joined Together" and "What Gets You Going." They were released on a 45 on the Bell Label out of New York.

Bob, Cliff and Ed later did a local release by The Tams, the same group that Cliff had under contract while in Atlanta. This record on Bob McRee's Passion Label included the songs "Hideway" and "Tell You For The Last Time."

They also wrote a song for Huey "Piano" Smith introducing a new dance called "The Popeye" which was released on Ace records.

Grits and Gravy Studio never released any music on its own label. They wrote songs, found artists to record their songs and leased the records to various labels across the country. They continued to do this well into the 1970's.

Upon closing the studio, they sold it to Mississippi College who turned it into a band hall.

The old Grits and Gravy Studio in Clinton, MS. Now the Mississippi College Band Hall.
(Photo by Bob Thayer)

BOB McREE, CLIFF THOMAS, ED THOMAS RECORDING STUDIO DISCOGRAPHY

Peggy Scott and Jo Jo Benson
Grits and Gravy Studio Clinton, MS
SSS736 *Lover's Holiday*
SSS International *Here With Me*

Peggy Scott and Jo Jo Benson
Grits and Gravy Studio Clinton, MS
SSS748 *Pickin' Wild Mountain Berries*
SSS International *Pure Love And Pleasure*

Mickey Murray and Clarence Murray
Grits and Gravy Studio Clinton, MS
SSS743 *How Do You Think I Can Live With Somebody*
SSS International *(After What I Been Used To)*

Joe Odom
Grits and Gravy Studio Clinton, MS
1710 *It's In Your Power*
123 Label *Big Love*

Johnny Copeland
Grits and Gravy Studio Clinton MS
45-2542 *It's My Own Tears That's Being Wasted*
Atlantic *Sufferin City*

Joe Odom
Grits and Gravy Studio Clinton, MS
P-1721 *Let Me Go Gradually*
123 Label *Think And Do*

The Chymes
Mississippi Artist Corp., Jackson, MS
7246-7246 Let's Try It Again
OKEH *Bring It Back Home*

Warren Storm
Grits and Gravy Studio Clinton, MS
6577-6577Rock Down In My Shoe
ATCO *Nobody Would Know*

Rod Bernard
Grits and Gravy Studio, Clinton, MS
In This Small Town
Copyright *Let's Start A Commotion*

Lavenia Lewis
Grits and Gravy Studio Clinton, MS
45-44048 *Tender Loving Pain*
Cotillion *Find A Man That Satisfies*

The Tams
Bill Lowery Productions, Atlanta, GA.
45-11228-A *Love, Love, Love*
ABC Records *Love Maker*

The Dolletts
Grits and Gravy Studio Clinton, MS
45-10625 *Small Talk (Doesn't Bother Me)*
Free From The Chains Of Love

The Tams
Grits and Gravy Studio Clinton, MS
P-123 *Hideway*
Passion *Tell You For The Last Times*

Peggy Scott
Grits and Gravy Studio Clinton, MS
73952 *Keepin' My Eye On You*
Mercury *Killing My Heart Again*

Peggy Scott
Grits and Gravy Studio Clinton, MS
6.12555 *You've Got It All*
Decca *Let Me Untie You*

Crowns
Grits and Gravy Studio Clinton, MS
3515-3515 *I Wonder Why*
Vee Jay *Better Luck*

Tommy (Tate) Yates
Grits and Gravy Studio Clinton, MS
VK-10556 *If You're Looking For A Fool*
Verve Records *Darling, Something's Gotta Give*

Otis Williams And The Charms
Grits and Gravy Studio Clinton, MS
7246-7247 *I Got Loving*
OKEH *Welcome Home*

Hank and Rover (Connie Davis and Tommy Tate)
Grits and Gravy Studio Clinton, MS
7264-7264 *A Rock Down In My Shoe*
OKEH *A Lot To Be Done*

Georgie Boy
Grits and Gravy Studio Clinton, MS
SSS-746 *The Pleasure Of My Woman*
SSS International *You'd Better Quit It*

Johnny W. Sumrall, Jr.

Fern Kinney
Grits and Gravy Studio Clinton, MS
2495-2495 Sweet Devil
Atlantic *Your Love's Not Reliable*

The Sugar Blues
Grits and Gravy Studio Clinton, MS
B-766 *Look What We Have Joined Together*
Bell Records *What Gets You Going*

Stephan
Muscle Shoals Sound Studios
STA-0130 *Wings And Wheels*
Stax Records *Keep On Loving Me*

TEEN TEMPOS

"Teen Tempos" was a television program on a local station in Jackson, Mississippi that was patterned after a show being run in Memphis, TN called "The Wink Martindale Show." I invited Chuck Allen, the producer of Teen Tempos, and Harriet McClure, a one-time hostess, to come on my radio show at WZRX to talk about how the show started and tell some of the things that happened on the show. They arrived at the station on that Saturday morning and the weather had been terrible the night before and the transmitter had been knocked out so we were not broadcasting. We did have electricity though so we went on and taped the show to be broadcast the following Saturday.

Chuck Allen was sent to Memphis by television station WLBT to check out "The Wink Martindale Dance Party Show." He checked into a local motel and turned on the T.V. to watch the show. It was a show featuring Wink doing a lot of talking with the teenagers dancing in the background to the music being played.

Upon his return to Jackson he had a discussion with the program director of WLBT, Maurice Thompson, and the station manager, Fred Beard. They decided to do a show with the teenagers doing more than just dancing in the background. It was decided they would feature a different high school each week. That high school would have four featured acts for the show and a teen report on what was going on at that particular school.

Chuck suggested a name for the show "Behind the Green Door". He envisioned the door opening and the camera rolling to where the teenagers were dancing to open the show. The phrase "behind the green door" came from a popular song of the day. Maurice Thompson and Fred Beard did not like that name so Chuck had to go back to the drawing board and he came up with the name "Teen Tempos."

On February 2, 1957, Teen Tempos was born. The first high school to appear was Murrah High School. The first show was somewhat of a disaster because of no rehearsal. Lou Ann Pepper became the first hostess for the show. She was attending Ole Miss at the time and would drive down on the weekend to do the show. Dick Crenshaw, the band director at Clinton High School, was the Music Director. Chuck Allen was the producer and selected the music to be played on the show. Since it was a family oriented show, Chuck was strict on the appearance of each teenager. If they were not properly dressed he would send them home to change clothes.

Teen Tempos provided a great place for local bands and statewide bands to appear. Andy Anderson and "The Rolling Stones;" Cliff Thomas (Ed and Barbara); and "Tim Whitsett and The Imperial Show Band" were just a few that appeared on the show.

Teen Tempos was on the air for 11 years and 552 shows. They went off the air in 1966. Some of the other hosts and hostesses over the years were: Hagan Thompson, Sandra Bailey, Nanette Workman and Judy Denson.

Below is a portion of the last song that Harriet McClure sang to Chuck Allen as Teen Tempos was going off the air for the last time. Chuck saved the cue cards.

"We will remember the years with you
The good days and the bad
Through it all,
The good times we had.

The high school kids, the ice cream cones,
The Pepsi's and the games,
The dancing couples filing by and somehow
The faces never matched the names.

But remember, all through the years,
The hours and the days,
We love you, Chuck,
We love you, Chuck,
In a million ways."

PEGGY PAXTON

Peggy Paxton started singing in high school and area talent shows in the late 50's and early 60's. Tim Whitsett heard her and decided to cut a record on her. In 1963 he took her into the Bob McRee's Bomac recording studio.

There they recorded “Somebody Somewhere”. It featured Peggy on vocals, Key Traylor on tenor sax, Tim Whitsett on organ, Alton Lott on guitar, Wray Hixson on bass, Dulin Lancaster on drums and The Del Sols on back up vocal. It was later released as a side to a Hank Martin release in 1964 entitled “I Would Cry”. She also worked in the early 60’s in various local clubs singing with Tim Whitsett and The Imperial Show Band.

In 1965-66 Peggy recorded eight songs at Phillips Studios in Memphis, TN. The songs were leased to Stan Lewis’ “Paula Record Label” in Shreveport, LA. Peggy made two appearances on the Louisiana Hayride in Shreveport. Her first record on Paula, “I Feel Like Crying” was heard by Jimmy Dean, which resulted in her appearing on his variety show in New York. After her appearance on that show she toured with Jimmy Dean throughout the country.

She married Wray Hixson, the bass player on her first record. Traveling and trying to raise a family became very difficult and after working locally around Jackson for a few more years, Peggy decided to retire from the music business in 1974. She and Wray now live in Shreveport, LA.

BOBBY J. MCCARTHY

Bobby J. McCarthy was an artist from the Laurel, Mississippi area who came to Jackson and played at a local club called "The Embers."

Bob McRee, a local record producer, was always looking for talent to sing his songs as well as songs written by Cliff and Ed Thomas. They got Bobby to come into the studios and record for them. One of the 45's they recorded on him was "Spoon It Up" and an old standard "If You Don't Know Me By Now". Bob released it locally on a label called Misty Blue Records.

They recorded two other 45's by him. One released on Pacemaker Records was "Who Ever Heard Of A Love Like This" and "Nobody's Child." The other release was on the 123 Label out of Atlanta, Georgia a division of Capitol Records headed up by Bill Lowery. The songs on that 45 were "Spoon Me Up Your Honey" and "Searching For The High Road."

Bobby went on to cut one more record for Ace Records which was a duet with Linda Calhoun called "It Has To Be Right" and "It Was The Best." I have been unable to locate any additional information on Linda Calhoun.

SHARI SCHNEIDER

Shari Schneider (late 1980's)

Shari was an on-air personality for local radio station WJDX in Jackson. She was an original "Gayfer Girl" for the department store and did their commercials and sang their jingles.

Bob McRee heard the commercials and invited Shari to record at his Nelson Street recording studio in Jackson. The first record consisted of re-makes of songs previously done by other artists and recorded by Bob and Cliff and Ed Thomas. The re-makes updated the tempo to make the songs sound fresh and new. One was a song originally recorded by Joe Odom entitled "Let Me Go Gradually" and the other song was "Flesh and Blood". Although the record was never released, it did get played on the radio.

When I was doing a radio show with Wayne Scott on WJDX in the late 1980's, I mentioned that I had a tape of the two songs. One day Wayne played them on air and surprised Shari. She couldn't believe I had them and that Wayne would play them. In my opinion, these are very good songs and should have been released.

Shari has also had a successful career in community theatre and is active in many projects in the metro-Jackson area today.

MALACO

The following is a brief history of MALACO Records of Jackson, Mississippi from several interviews with Gerald "Wolf" Stephenson.

Malaco started as a partnership between two brothers-in-law Mitch Malouf and Tommy Couch as a company focused on booking musical acts. Somewhere along the way Wolf Stephenson bought out Mitch. They evolved into a recording studio when Wolf came on board.

Wolf owned The Zodiac Club in Mart 51, a shopping center on Terry Road in Jackson. He had just remodeled the club and had started bringing in bands to play every night. One of the first bands he brought in was a group named "The CrackerJacks."

Wolf graduated from The University of Mississippi, "Ole Miss" in Oxford, Mississippi and had been a member of a fraternity. On several occasions the fraternity would have a tea dance and invite a performer named Mississippi Fred McDowell from Como, Mississippi to perform. He was a blues artist who traveled all over the United States and Europe to many blues festivals and often was the featured performer. He worked at the Stuckey's in Como,

Mississippi and when they wanted him to perform they would call him there.

Wolf and Tommy were asked to record another blues singer in their studio and after they completed the album on this other artist they thought of Fred and thought he sounded better so they decided to record Fred. They called the Stuckey's and got Fred to come and make an album. The records Fred had made previously were only 45's and were recorded by guys recording Fred singing and playing on the front porch of his house - not in a recording studio. Wolf and Tommy leased the album Mississippi Fred McDowell to Capital Records and it went on to be nominated for a Grammy in 1969.

There was one particular recording session that Wolf told me about when several groups came from New Orleans in taxicabs. They came one weekend and recorded the music and the next weekend came and recorded the vocals. They were very well organized and out of that recording session came two hit records. The man who had the music all organized was Wardell Quezergue.

The first record was by "King Floyd." Tommy and Wolf shopped it around to some of the major labels of the time but no one wanted to take a chance on it so they decided to press it themselves. They put it out on the Chimmeyville label, named after the name given Jackson, Mississippi after the Civil War. The A-side to King Floyd's record was "What Our Love Needs" and the B-side was "Groove Me". A DJ in New Orleans for some unknown reason played the B-side "Groove Me" one day and the phone lines lit up and the requests starting pouring in - it was an instant hit. One of the record companies, Atlantic Records, that had previously turned down the song called them and they worked out a distribution deal with them. This was Malaco's first Gold Record.

Also out of that same recording session came Jean Knight's recording of "Mister Big Stuff" which was only released on an album which was leased to Stax Records.

Another song that was a big success for Malaco was Dorothy Moore's "Misty Blue." Joe Simon originally recorded the song and it was a regional hit for him. Wolf and Tommy liked it from their college days at Ole Miss. They decided to get Dorothy to record it. She had done some other recordings for them and had also done some backup work. It was a year and a half before they decided to shop it around to some major labels along with some other songs that they had recorded by other artists; and they got the same reaction they had gotten on the King

Floyd song. The comment they got on Dorothy's song was "that it was a slow ballad by a black female and it won't get played." They came back to Jackson and decided to press a few copies like they did on King Floyd and release them to the radio stations and see if they would play the song. A DJ in Chicago started playing it and it became an instant hit and won a Gold Record for them. "Misty Blue" was the first Gold Record on the Malaco Label.

Another story that Wolf told me was when Carson Whitsett was in the studio jamming with some of the studio musicians one day and Wolf was on the control panel. They starting playing a particular song and he liked it so he decided to record it. The song was an instrumental and had no name. Wolf said it sounded like a dog wandering down an alley looking for food or some trouble to get into in the middle of the night. So he named it "Dog In The Night". It was released as a single on the Malaco label in 1974.

ZZ Hill came to Malaco after being on several small record labels. He was a real well known rhythm and blues singer. The major label that he previously was on, Columbia, had just dropped him because his sales had dropped below what they wanted. Malaco did an album on him and did not release a 45 as other labels had done in the past. The first two songs on the album became instant hits. They were "Down Home Blues" and "Cheating In The Next Room". The album stayed on Billboard's 'Top Hit Chart" for sixteen weeks, which was unheard of at the time for a rhythm and blues album. This album was released in 1980.

Another group that recorded at Malaco was "Sho-Nuff." They were popular locally, but were more popular in Japan. Malaco recorded an album by them and released it entitled "Stand Up For Love." Group members were Lyn Chambers, James Lewis, Lawrence Lewis, Bruce Means and Freddie Young. One song from the album, "Don't Be Lonely," was a regional hit.

The local band, "The CrackerJacks," also recorded at Malaco. "The CrackerJacks" consisted of Don Barrett, Johnny Barranco, Steve Featherston, Sergio Fernandez, Hugh Garraway, Perry Lomax and Keith Marsalis. They released an album on Chimmeyville Records of their most requested songs being played at Wolf Stephenson's Zodiac Club at Mart 51 on Terry Road in Jackson, Mississippi.

Wolf and Tommy also released a 12-inch disco record using a local artist, Fern Kinney. Fern had sung with Dorothy Moore in a group and sang back up with several other artists. They choose a previously recorded song recorded by King Floyd "Groove Me" and set to a disco beat. It did well regionally but was not a nation-wide hit.

Another local artist that was in the studio band at the recording studio was Jerry Puckett. Wolf and Tommy decided to do a record on him. It was entitled "Hallelujah" and released on the 123 Label, a label used by Bill Lowery. It did real well locally but not nation-wide.

Two guys who came from Meridian, Mississippi to record were George Soule, who was a local DJ there, and Paul Davis. Up until this time, Malaco had only been a recording studio but with this duo they got into actually doing production work on a record. George and Paul were songwriters and singers. Wolf and Tommy did a lot of demos for them. A lady named Ilene Burns from Bang records came from New York one day to hear some other artists that Malaco had and heard some of Paul Davis's music and signed him to a contract and he left and went to New York. His biggest hit on Bang Records was "Mississippi River" and "Who's Gonna Love Me Tomorrow." Wolf and Tommy realized that they had all the demos that Paul had done for them and knew that if they didn't put them out in a certain length of time they would lose the right to them. They quickly pressed the songs on an album with no jacket entitled "Paul's Friends Sing Paul's Songs" on a label that said "Surprise Records." Jerry Puckett, a studio musician at Malaco, overdubbed most of the songs and they released it. Wolf and Tommy took it around to some of the local record stores and told them to sell it for what they could get for it.

Wolf and Tommy went on to release some of Paul's original songs on the Tetragrammaton Record Label. George Soule was the singer on these songs. Paul Davis wrote one side of the record "Mississippi River" and Paul and George wrote the other side "Talkin' About Love".

Another local release album that was recorded at Malaco was an album by two guys who came from Greenville, Mississippi to the Zodiac Club, Jimmy Wright and Will Hegman. Will had a dream of being a record producer and songwriter and he had a friend named Jimmy Wright who could also sing and write songs. Will was hoping someone would decide to record some of his and Jimmy's songs. They came into the studio and recorded an album using the name "Fuzzy Buffer." One of the songs on the album was titled "Midnight On The Delta." Of course Midnight is the name of a town in the Mississippi delta. Wolf and Tommy put the album out on the Copasetic

Label. Another song on the album was "She's A Part Of You." The album was a limited release and the sales were very minimal. The album was recorded in 1975. They also cut two songs during this period as demos and had them pressed on to a 45 and used a label called the Reject records. The two songs were "Lovin' Eyes" and "Hard Times". Malaco only pressed a few records and called them unreleased masters.

Another artist that recorded at Malaco was G.C. Cameron from McComb, Mississippi. He had been with the nationally known group "The Spinners." Malaco released an album on him entitled "Give Me Your Love." One song that came out of that album became a standard at high school graduations and high school reunions - "So Hard To Say Goodbye To Yesterday."

McKinley Mitchell was another artist who came to Malaco. He had hits on other record labels. Malaco recorded an album on him and released it on the Chimmeyville Record Label. One of the songs that was a big hit on the album was a remake of an old Bobby Darin song "Dream Lover."

Malaco released several albums on a local artist, Tommy Tate, to the Japanese market that were never released in the United States. A group of Japanese rhythm and blues fans would come by the studio from time to time and listen to demos that were available. Carson Whitsett and Tommy Tate were constantly in the studio writing songs together and recording these songs. The Japanese liked the songs and put up the money for Malaco to make these albums and release them in Japan. One of these albums was "Hold On" by Tommy Tate.

Another album Malaco released only in Japan under the same circumstances was an album called "Soul Chant" by Soul Brothers & A Soul Sister. This featured Betty Johnson, Charles Warren, Patterson Twins and The Fiesta's.

In about 1975 Andy Anderson was living on the Mississippi Gulf Coast and had been out of the music business for a while. He came into the studio and wanted to cut a record. J. J. Hettinger, III, a fellow musician that he was working with in a band on the coast accompanied him. J.J. had written two songs and wanted Andy to sing with him on the record. They came into the studio and recorded "Long, Long Way To Go" and "Rhonda". They used the names "Eagle and Hawk." "Hawk" was a nickname for J.J. who was an English teacher on the coast and Andy took on the name of "Eagle." Malaco released the songs on a

45 record on the Aerie Record Label out of Santa Fe, New Mexico. It enjoyed some limited success.

This has been a brief look at Malaco Records through the eyes of Wolf Stephenson in three interviews that I did with him. Malaco Records now specializes in rhythm and blues and black gospel music.

MALACO DISCOGRAPHY

Music recorded at Malaco recording studio during the period covered in Classic Magnolia Rock. These songs were either released on the Malaco label, the Chimmneyville label or leased to other labels as noted.

Mississippi Fred McDowell
"I do not play no rock'n'roll"
Album recorded at Malaco, but leased to Capitol Records.

The CrackerJacks
"Mississippi Home Grown" recorded at Malaco, released on Chimneyville Records, featuring:
Don Barrett (bass, organ, piano, lead vocals, percussion),
Johnny Barranco (Lead vocals, guitar, bass percussion),
Steve Featherston (drums, vocals),
Sergio Fernandez (organ, piano, drums, vocals),
Hugh Garraway (tenor sax, alto sax),
Perry Lomax (trumpet, percussion), and
Keith Marsalis (lead guitar, vocals).

King Floyd
"King Floyd"
recorded at Malaco, released on Chimneyville Records, released as an album and as a single 45, the A-side *"Woman Don't Go Astray"* and the B-side *"Groove Me."*

Jean Knight
"Mr. Big Stuff"
recorded at Malaco leased to Stax records.

Dorothy Moore
"Misty Blue"
recorded at Malaco, released on Malaco Records.

Johnny W. Sumrall, Jr.

Carson Whitsett
"A Dog In The Night"
recorded at Malaco, released on Malaco Records as a 45.

Z. Z. Hill
"Down Home"
recorded at Malaco, released on Malaco Records as an album only. Featured two of his best know hits *"Down Home Blues"* and *"Cheating In The Next Room."*

Sho-Nuff
"Stand Up For Love"
recorded at Malaco, released on Malaco Records as an album only. Features: Lyn Chambers, James Lewis, Lawrence Lewis, Bruce Means and Freddie Young. Best known song on album: *"Don't Be Lonely."*

Fern Kinney
"Groove Me"
12 inch disco record recorded at Malaco and released on Malaco Records.

Jerry Puckett
"Hallelujah" and *"All I'm Living For"*
recorded at Malaco and leased to 123 Records as a 45 record.

George Soule
"Talkin' About Love" and *"Mississippi River"* recorded at Malaco and leased to Tetragrammaton Records as a 45.

Paul Davis
"Paul's Friends Sing Paul's Songs"
recorded at Malaco and released on Surprise Records.

Fuzzy Buffer
"Copasetic"
recorded at Malaco and released on the Copasetic Record label. It featured Jimmy Wright singing songs that he had written and some songs that he and Will Hegman had written.

Fuzzy Buffer
"Hard Times" and *"Lovin' Eyes"*
recorded at Malaco on the Reject Label, but never released.

G. C. Cameron
"Give Me Your Love"
recorded at Malaco, released by Malaco Records. Featured his hit song *"So Hard To Say Goodbye To Yesterday."*

McKinley Mitchell
"McKinley Mitchell"
recorded at Malaco, released by Chimneyville Records as an album only.

Tommy Tate
"Hold On"
recorded at Malaco, only released by Malaco Records in Japan as an album.

Soul Brothers and Soul Sister
"Soul Chant"
recorded by Malaco, only released by Malaco Records in Japan as an album. Features: Betty Johnson, Charles Warren, Patterson Twins, and The Fiesta's.

CLASSIC MAGNOLIA ROCK CD CONTENTS and ORDER FORM

A compilation CD of the following songs is available from the author. This CD has the proper Master Use License and Mechanical Licenses for each of the recordings by Harry Fox Agency, Inc. and other sources. You may purchase the CD from the author by using the order form at the end of this list.

1. Swanee River Rock ---The Red Tops
   Writer: Huddleston
   Publisher: Unknown

2. Please Be Mine---The Vels
   Writers: Caldwell, Evans, Knight, and Sanders
   Publisher: Whitsett Brothers Music BMI

3. Johnny Valentine---Andy Anderson and
   The Original Rolling Stones
   Writers: Anderson, Tubb
   Publisher: Murray Nash Assoc. BMI

4. I-I-I Love You---Andy Anderson and
   The Original Rolling Stones
   Writers: Anderson, Tubb
   Publisher: Buna Music Corp BMI

5. You Shake Me Up---Andy Anderson and
   The Original Rolling Stones
   Writer: Anderson
   Publisher: Buna Music Corp BMI

6. Little Liza Jane---Tim Whitsett
   Writers: Tim Whitsett
   Publisher: Whitsett Brothers Music BMI

7. Stand By Me---Tommy Tate
   Writers: King, Lieber, and Stoller
   Publisher: Sony ATV Songs BMI

8. All I Need---Hank and Buzz
   Writer: Tim Whitsett
   Publisher: Whitsett Brothers Music BMI

9. Sorry I Lied---Cliff Thomas (Ed and Barbara)
   Writer: Ed Thomas Jr.
   Publisher: Knox Music Inc. BMI

10. Send Me A Little Girl ---Wendell Moore
    Writers: Jimmy Hodo, Bob McRee
    Publisher: Whitsett Brothers Music BMI

11. Shame---Cliff and Ed Thomas
    Writers: Cliff and Ed Thomas.
    Publisher: Ace Pub. Co. BMI

12. That's What I'll Do----Bubba Jordan
    Writer: Jordan
    Publisher: Whitsett Brothers Music BMI

13. Tough, Tough, Tough ---Andy Anderson and The Dawnbreakers
    Writers: Andy Anderson
    Publisher: Singing River Pub. BMI

14. Promise Me---Andy Anderson and The Dawnbreakers
    Writers: Andy Anderson
    Publisher: Buna Pub. BMI

15. A Wish For Love --- Ron Fraiser
    Writers: Jordan
    Publisher: Fraiser Music Co. BMI

16. Macks By The Tracks ---Tim Whitsett
Writers: Tim Whitsett
Whitsett Brothers Music BMI

17. Ring On Your Finger --- Glenn Sutton
Writers: Sutton, McRee
Publisher: Ace Pub. BMI

18. Down The Aisle --- Jimmy Clanton and
Mary Ann Mobley
Writers: Norwood, Brandel
Publisher: Miller Music BMI

19. Waiting For The Sun To Go Down—
Buddy Rogers
Writer: Bob McRee
Publisher: Low-Thom Music BMI

20. Gimme Lock A Yo Hair---Andy Anderson and
The Dawnbreakers
Writer: Andy Anderson
Publisher: Singing River Pub. BMI

21. Tell Her Mister Moon ---Al Ward
Writers: Vidacovich, Bolte
Publisher: Miller Music ASCAP

22. Unfaithful Love ---Terry Dee and
The Road Runners
Writers: Terry Dunn
Publisher: Whitsett Brothers Music BMI

CLASSIC MAGNOLIA ROCK CD
ORDER FORM

Quantity	Cost/each	Total
	$14.00	

The cost of the CD is $10.76 plus 7% Mississippi State Sales Tax plus $2.49 Shipping and Handling per CD.

Send a money order or cashiers check to:

Johnny W. Sumrall Jr.
769 Highpoint Drive
Byram, MS 39272

Allow 10-14 business days for delivery.

Johnny Sumrall on WZRX (1987).
(Photo by Sandy Ates)

JOHNNY SUMRALL

Johnny Sumrall is a native of Jackson, MS and is a graduate of Provine High School and Belhaven College. His love of music crosses all genres, but is focused on Rock and Roll. This book is a compilation of his memories as a teenager during the era as well as information from interviews with the artists. Many of the artists are good friends with whom Johnny stays in contact.

Johnny produced and hosted a live radio program "Original Mississippi Rock and Roll Music" during the late 1980's and early 1990's which featured many of the artists in interviews as well as performing their music. He has written articles for VIP Magazine and contributed to the book All Shook Up – Mississippi Roots of American Popular Music by Christina Wilson.

He and his wife live in Byram, MS and are the parents of three sons and five grandchildren. You may contact him at jsum402@earthlink.net.

Printed in the United States
129234LV00002B/2/P

9 781438 929606